THIRSTING
FOR GOD
IN A LAND OF SHALLOW WELLS

BY MATTHEW GALLATIN

Ancient Faith Publishing
Chesterton, Indiana

Published by   Ancient Faith Publishing
                    (formerly known as Conciliar Press)
                    (A division of Ancient Faith Ministries)
                    P.O. Box 748
                    Chesterton, IN 46304

Printed in the United States of America

ISBN 978-1-888212-28-0

Unless otherwise noted, all Scripture quotations are from
the New King James Version of the Bible, © 1982
by Thomas Nelson, Inc., Nashville, Tennessee
and are used by permission.

Front cover design by Mark Wainwright, Symbology Creative

Contents

Introduction

This book is written for people who have but one ultimate desire—to be in love with God. More specifically, I could say it is for evangelical Protestants who have devoted their lives to finding an intimate relationship with God. But most especially, it is for those sincere but often misunderstood souls who have been willing to lay aside doctrinal and denominational allegiance in their devoted quest for that mysterious "something"—that indefinable element of true faith for which they long, but which no church, doctrine, or teacher has ever been able to place within their outstretched hands.

I was one of those folks. And I have known many, many others.

In my encounters with these kindred spirits, it was not unusual for our conversation eventually to come around to the early Church. We would reflect with almost romantic wistfulness over the powerful faith of the Apostles and martyrs. Within their souls, Jesus created a world that transcends this one. How we yearned for Him to live in our hearts just as He lived in theirs. We wanted Him to use us to turn the world "upside down" (Acts 17:6). The secret to that kind of experience was what we were longing to find.

Yes, we spoke much of the early Church. But we really knew almost nothing about it. We'd never read any early history of the Church; we didn't think that was necessary. After all, we all knew that after that first glorious generation of the Apostles, the Church had become a ship set upon by piratical heresies, run aground by deceived pilots. The true faith of the Apostles had not been restored until Martin Luther and the other Reformers reclaimed it from centuries of abuse.

But we were searching for something yet undiscovered, something even the Reformers hadn't completely grasped or handed on to us. Somehow, we all knew it was back there, in that glorious time before the Church's dismal descent into spiritual error. But for all our intensive mining of the Scriptures, not one of us had uncovered that gem of truth. Sometimes we thought we had; but in time, we'd discover that the gem was only colored glass.

Then in my early forties, I faced a moment of truth. For the very first time in my life, I seriously considered this simple question: If the people of Christ are one undivided Body, as St. Paul says, why are there so many different versions of the truth? How can Bible-believing Protestants look at the very same Scriptures and come up with so many different doctrinal statements, so many different pictures of God? Is this the way it's supposed to be?

For the first time, I looked at some obvious facts and began to put two and two together. What I realized at that momentous turning point in my life was this: the way of Protestant faith could never lead me to that essential truth for which my friends and I so earnestly sought. To my amazement, this was an inescapable conclusion, and very easily reached. How I arrived at it is the subject of the first four chapters of this book.

When I say that this discovery plunged me into the darkest moments of my life, I do not exaggerate. It shook me to my roots. After all, I'd been born into a Bible-believing Protestant home. I'd given my whole adult life to evangelical Protestant ministry, as a pastor, counselor, teacher, and musician. But thanks be to God, my redemption from that dark time lifted me to places of light that I could never have foreseen. For in climbing out from the shadows of an old faith, I at last found it—the way back to the early Church!

I must confess that the nature of that path home surprised me. It turns out that what connects me to that wondrous early Church is not a hidden doctrine or spiritual principle. Instead, it is a living link. You see, the Church of the Apostles never actually disappeared! It did not collapse under the weight of heresies. It did not retreat to some remote mountain valley or desert, to be preserved by a tiny esoteric cult. Neither did it hide itself in revelatory darkness, awaiting a distant age when some gifted theologian would resurrect it with a secret key to the Scriptures.

No, I discovered that every belief and practice of that wondrous Church of the Apostles is preserved to this day in a body of believers that is two hundred and fifty million strong—second only to the Roman Catholic Church in size. It continues to be the Church of martyrs; millions of its members have been martyred in the twentieth century alone. But in the beauty and truth of the Holy Spirit it stands, faithfully fulfilling the commandment of the Apostle Paul:

> Therefore, brethren, *stand fast and hold the traditions which you were taught,* whether by word or our epistle (2 Thessalonians 2:15, italics mine).

The very same traditions that were in the mind of the Apostle Paul as he penned those words twenty centuries ago still light the way and mark the path of this Church. The devoted faithful of this Church walk with Christ in an intimate love that transcends the world. In the blessed embrace of this Church, I found that mysterious "something" that I'd sought for all my life. That, and spiritual blessings I never imagined, I encountered within the Church that opened its doors at Pentecost—the Holy Eastern Orthodox Church.

Now, Protestants in this country are relatively uninformed when it comes to the Orthodox Church. Many know nothing of it at all. Nevertheless, the *Encyclopedia Britannica* has recognized the Orthodox Church as the fastest-growing church in America today.[1] I'll relate how I came to discover this ancient Faith in Chapters 5 and 6.

I had abandoned Protestantism because of certain inherent defects I had identified in its roots. But in the light of Orthodoxy, I began to see that the flaws and inadequacies of Protestant faith run even deeper than I had previously recognized. I'm not talking here about troubles with specific doctrines in particular denominations. Rather, I'm speaking of problems that undermine *every* Protestant's faith—regardless of his denomination, "nondenomination," or sect. Part II of this book will address these difficulties.

Having once been in their shoes, I know my Protestant readers may find these problems challenging to face. But they may be equally challenged by the remaining chapters of the book, in which I attempt to offer a taste of the Faith of the first Christians, as it has been preserved in the Orthodox Church. It may be hard for them to entertain the thought that doctrines and practices they deem "unscriptural" were actually seen as perfectly scriptural by the people to whom the New Testament documents were written.

Of course, I'm not the only Protestant who's discovered these truths. Literally thousands of American Protestants (in some cases, entire congregations of them) in recent years have come home to their ancient roots. These newcomers recognize in Orthodox Christianity the beauty of the early Church. They are ready to embrace its spiritual vitality wholeheartedly.

One great blessing is that with the arrival of these new Protestant converts on the doorsteps of their previously isolated churches, many self-confessed nominal Orthodox are rediscovering their Faith! When they encounter people who have come to the ancient Faith for the Faith's sake, they begin to ask themselves, "What is it that I possess here, anyway?" Thus the embers that have lain cold in many hearts are now being rekindled with holy fire.

Orthodoxy is receiving such broad acceptance today not because it is strange, or exotic, or Eastern, or new. No, it is simply the *truth*. It is the Faith that began changing the universe two thousand years ago, and it has never waned.

This book is the story of my journey into this ancient Faith. Here, my life with God exceeds all I ever dreamed. Today, the words "I love Jesus" hold a meaning for me that I cannot fully express to a Protestant who does not share my Orthodox frame of reference. But one who will read this book prayerfully, patiently, and thoughtfully may, by the time he or she reaches its final pages, catch a blessed glimpse of the Christ who sheds His wondrous love upon His faithful, in the light of Holy Orthodoxy.

Part I

The Heart
of the Matter

Looking for the Truth

One spring day when I was nine years old, I became aware of Jesus Christ. I don't mean I came to believe in Him that day. No, I don't think there was ever a time that I didn't believe in Him. A dirt-poor Appalachian farm boy learns early to depend on the name Jesus, for everything from a good crop to his next meal.

But on that day, I was thinking about His love, His goodness, and how much I wanted to do His will. Suddenly, in a moment both fearful and joyous, I felt His Presence. In a powerfully quiet, peaceful, all-encompassing way, Jesus was suddenly more real to me than anything or anyone. I couldn't fathom what was happening inside me. All I could think to do was run to the house, sit down at our old upright piano, and do my little-boy best to write a hymn.

What I'd had, of course, was what evangelical Protestants commonly refer to as a "conversion experience." I was wrapped in that divine warmth often referred to as "first love." Jesus was now much more than the wondrous Name to whom I addressed my prayers. He was more than the beloved Hero of my cherished Bible stories. Now, He was my ever-present God—and Friend.

He was with me later that same spring, when I carelessly stuck my hand down a hole in the ground and was bitten by a hidden snake. At first I panicked. Was it a rattlesnake or a copperhead? We were thirty miles from the nearest doctor. If it was something poisonous, my life was in danger.

But to this day, my mother likes to tell people that by the time they got me loaded into the car, I was completely calm. "If Jesus wants me to die," I told her, "then that's okay." Whether the snake was poisonous or not, we never knew for sure; but I never suffered any ill effects from the bite.

In the late summer of that same year, Jesus saw me through one of the most heartbreaking moments of my life. My grandfather, the best and dearest friend any boy could ever have, passed away one August morning at dawn. My father awakened me to tell me the tragic news. I got up and ran to the barn, crying my eyes out. But there in the hayloft, Jesus came to me and calmed me. "Dad-dad" was with Him now, and that thought mingled joy with my grieving tears.

So when I was a child, my life with Christ revolved around a simple awareness of His Presence. Being near to Him was not a hard thing to achieve. I had no thought for theology or doctrine. There was simply the blessed *Jesus*, always abiding closely and lovingly.

The Age of Reasons
But as I grew older, I was taught that faith in Christ is a more complex issue than I had imagined. I was told that a person's godliness is really measured by the truth of his doctrine. There are theological questions that must be answered correctly, and problems of biblical interpretation that must be solved. I was of a temperament that found these intellectual challenges most exciting. I'm sure that's why I didn't notice my first love fading. Subtly, the living Jesus who was simply *there* was being replaced by a theological portrait. But the Christ of my childhood would return one day; and on that day, my life would change forever.

My love affair with theology began when I was twelve. My family was rescued from dire financial straits by a kind and loving Seventh-Day Adventist family. We hadn't known them long before they invited us to attend some Bible studies at their home on Friday evenings.

For the first time, I was introduced to serious Bible study. The Scripture lessons were on filmstrips, with an accompanying reel-to-reel tape. I was smitten—not just by the "high-tech" presentations, but by the whole idea that Jesus, and the things He wanted me to believe and do, were revealed clearly on the pages of that ancient Book. My intellectual powers were beginning to blossom, and I found this business of discovering the real Christ through study completely fascinating.

Over the next few months, I devoured that Book. My parents and I came to believe that what the Bible taught about Christian faith was different from what we had practiced before. I also learned that one must be able to defend what he believes when questioned, to show from the Scriptures the undeniable truth of one's doctrine. My parents and I were convinced that Seventh-Day Adventism was the true path to God, and we were prepared to stand up for it. In December of my thirteenth year, we joined the church.

Throughout my high school years, I avidly studied my newfound faith. I had every doctrine down pat. I knew all the scriptural arguments. The trials that come from not going to dances or movies and worshiping on a different day from other Christians (Adventists observe the Saturday Sabbath), I bore faithfully.

When I graduated from high school, I headed off to an Adventist college to study for the ministry. To know Jesus better was my one desire. Serving Him was all I could imagine doing with my life. By this point in time, I understood well that such a commitment would require intense effort. The Bible was full of things that I didn't know yet. I needed to unlock its secret treasures.

True to my hopes, college brought exciting theological discoveries. I loved my professors and hung on every word of their learned teaching. These men filled the longing in my soul, my deep thirst for the knowledge of God.

Then one day in my second-year theology class, my rosy world was disturbed. We were studying the Adventist belief that Christians must observe the Levitical distinction between clean and unclean meats (Leviticus 11). At some point in our discussion, my favorite professor told us we needed to accept the fact that this doctrine "is very difficult to defend from a purely scriptural standpoint." There are just too many biblical passages, he observed, that appear to refute it. When we looked carefully at those scriptures, I decided he was right. He advised us that as Adventist theologians, we should rather condemn meat-eating altogether. After all, he reminded us, vegetarianism is the more "pure" and more "spiritual" Adventist view.

It can easily be argued as the diet God originally intended for mankind. The first chapter of Genesis makes it clear Adam and Eve were given only fruits, grains, and vegetables to eat.

All this was hard for me to hear, especially since I wasn't a vegetarian! The filmstrips had taught me that according to the Bible, eating meat was okay, so long as it wasn't pork or shellfish. Now, this professor was telling me that the Book isn't crystal clear on that matter. I was troubled by this possibility. After all, I had come to bank on the biblical certainty of my doctrine. Believing what is right, I'd been taught, is what connects a person to Christ.

The whole experience troubled and confused me. I dealt with it by convincing myself that the problem would disappear if I kept studying. Adventism was the truth, I was sure. Eventually, I'd be able to explain this apparent weakness in its theology. I wouldn't let a little issue like meat-eating derail my spiritual life.

The Turning Point

Adverse circumstances forced me to leave college before I had attained my degree in theology—a turn of events for which, in retrospect, I am extremely grateful. My commitment to Christ and to my church, however, did not wane. At age twenty-three, I found myself working as the lay assistant to the area-wide Adventist youth director of a large city. In that capacity, I taught the youth class at one of the local churches on Saturday mornings.

Early one Saturday, I was preparing an in-depth study on some doctrinal issue. As I pored over a point, trying to come up with a way to make it clear to a bunch of sixteen-year-olds, a question veritably erupted in my soul. Without warning, and as distinctly as if someone were speaking, it came: *Do you know what you believe?*

"Of course." I remember that I shocked myself by answering out loud. The question was that demanding. Equally surprising was the instantaneous reply: *Yes, you know what you believe. But is it the truth?*

I can still recall how those words rang in my mind. Yet infinitely more powerful than the words was the beautiful, long-forgotten Presence that surrounded me in that moment—the same one I had felt when I was a little boy. I began to weep with remembrance, with humility, with repentance, with love, and with joy. In an instant, the Jesus of my childhood swept aside all the theological veils that I had woven around my heart. Once again, He was simply *there*. How wonderful it was to feel His touch!

But the years had done me damage. I guess I didn't know how to be a child anymore. His Presence soon faded from my awareness. All I was left with was that question ringing in my soul: *Is what you believe the truth?*

It is tempting for me to look back upon that moment and wish that God had made me aware right then of all the beautiful things I know today. It would have saved me nearly thirty years of stumbling and struggle on my way to discovering the answer to that question. But in His love, His mercy, and His divine purpose, our beloved Christ decided that my journey to Truth must be a longer one.

Still, Jesus had at that moment reawakened me. I recognized that what I really longed for in my life was that immediate awareness of His Presence. He had also left me with that question. Somehow, my heart knew that when I discovered the truth, I would rediscover, in a powerful and abiding way, my childlike first love. But before that could happen, I had much to learn—or, as it turned out, to unlearn.

A New Path

On that particular Saturday morning, I was filled with resolve. Nagging little doubts that had been accumulating since that disturbing day in theology class could no longer be suppressed. I had taken the truth of my doctrine for granted. Now, I knew that I must test it.

I devised a course of action. I would put away all my Adventist books and commentaries. Armed only with my King James Bible and my *Strong's Concordance*, I would reinvestigate my doctrines. There was a problem here, though. I knew only one way to interpret Scripture—the Adventist way. To challenge it, I needed a different doctrinal viewpoint with which to compare it. Of the non-Adventist preachers I'd heard on television and radio, the ones who made the best impression on me were those who referred to themselves as "fundamentalists." So I decided to weigh my Adventist theology against theirs, to see whose understanding actually squared better with the Scriptures.

For five intense years, I followed this course. The doctrines that had been pillars of my Adventist faith one by one tottered and fell. What the fundamentalist Protestants taught seemed to me much simpler, more sensible, more consistent, and above all, more reflective of the loving Christ who is revealed in the Gospels.

These were extremely difficult years for me. I can't tell you how many nights I awoke in a cold sweat, shuddering in the awful fear that I might be committing apostasy. But there were other very special nights, nights with the Presence of Christ. Especially, there was the morning I was awakened at two o'clock by a command to go look at a passage of Scripture and "read what it does not say." Following that order freed me from all my questions and concerns about the necessity of seventh-day Sabbath worship.

The Sabbath requirement was the last bastion of my Adventist faith. When it toppled in the light of the Scriptures, it was as if an infinite weight had been lifted from my shoulders. I was certain that a new day had dawned for me. Surely now, nothing stood between me and the truth—between me and the rediscovery of an abiding, heartfelt awareness of Christ.

Where Is Love?

Thus I began a new journey, this time among the Protestant fundamentalists. Their uncompromising commitment to truth and their willingness to take the Bible "as it reads" had won my admiration and respect. But it wasn't long before I learned that Sunday-keeping Protestants have their own set of doctrinal squabbles. A host of antithetical terms—like *Calvinist, Arminian, dispensation, covenant, pre-Tribulation,* and *post-Tribulation*—became part of my vocabulary. I discovered that my work of studying and choosing from among doctrines was in no wise over. I buckled down and kept at it.

One important topic of theological debate particularly interested me—the whole business of spiritual gifts. As an Adventist, I'd been taught that charismatics are dangerously off-base. My new fundamentalist friends agreed. But I saw in the charismatics a heartfelt spiritual liveliness I didn't see in my fundamentalist environment. Oh, we prayed to Jesus, sang to Him, worshiped Him, and studied the Bible with unparalleled intensity. But I wasn't finding there the "Jesus of the heart" whom I so desperately longed to rediscover. In fact, I remember remarking to my wife, Alice, one day after church: "This feels just like Adventism, only on Sundays."

Then one Thursday night, a musician friend with whom I often performed encouraged me to attend a service at his charismatic church. To soften any reluctance, my friend assured me that his was a "quietly charismatic" church. He told me that the folks there believed in spiritual gifts like heavenly languages, prophecy, and healing, but they practiced them in a well-managed, low-key way. He introduced me to the term *afterglow*, that time at the end of the regular service when those who so wished could stay and worship using their spiritual gifts. My friend said I wouldn't have to stay. But if I did, I'd see that this "worship in the Spirit" followed the Apostle Paul's guidelines for orderliness in worship (1 Corinthians 14).

Alice and I had come to a point where we were ready to investigate these things for ourselves. So we took the chance and went. Almost immediately, we recognized something intriguing there that we hadn't encountered in the fundamentalist churches. The place had a certain spiritual warmth, an inviting atmosphere of devotion. We felt it in the way the people sang with their eyes blissfully closed and their hands upraised. It showed in the simplicity of the music—choruses taken mostly from the Psalms, accompanied by a single guitar. It came through clearly in the passionate preaching of the pastor, who had long hair, wore blue jeans, explained Bible passages verse by verse, and talked from the heart about life with God in the real world.

At the end of the service came the afterglow. As my friend had promised, it was calm and orderly. Some people in the congregation started to share what they called "words from the Lord." These were messages of admonition and encouragement. Some were directed to the church as a whole; others were given to specific individuals. Alice and I were confused and overwhelmed, trying to figure out what to make of all this unusual stuff.

Then the pastor, his eyes closed, his expression rapt, said, "There is a young couple here tonight who have been on a spiritual journey. You've come out of a strange sect. You haven't really found what you're looking for spiritually. God wants you to know that you've found your home here."

An electrical jolt went straight through me. Alice and I turned toward each other, tears streaming down our cheeks. We both were certain that God was talking about us. From that night, we began attending that church.

It quickly became clear to me that within the charismatic realm, I stood a much better chance of finding my "heart connection" with Christ than I did among the fundamentalists. But what about the other aspect of my commitment—my devotion to doctrinal purity? I soon learned that the charismatics were just as committed to biblical truth as were the fundamentalists. They only practiced the gifts, after all, because the Bible instructs that they be practiced. Those charismatic Bible teachers with whom I became acquainted were some of the most serious Bible students I'd ever known.

Eventually, I became the music minister in a mission church that our congregation established. Within a year, I became the mission's pastor. I vigorously devoted myself to the charismatic life. I was certain that this path would lead to the goal that I had set for myself long before: *to know that what I believe is the undeniable truth, and to find that truth transforming my life through the powerful inner Presence of our Lord Jesus Christ.*

→ 2 ←

Warning Signs

S ometimes I think I might still be a charismatic, were it not for the fact that I was also a pastor. Being the man in charge, however, eventually compelled me to look hard at my charismatic experiences. I was forced to question the spiritual validity of the life I was leading and teaching others to embrace.

I do believe to this day that some of the things that occurred in those charismatic gatherings were the bona fide work of God. I think especially of certain acts of the Holy Spirit that resulted in profound, life-changing repentance. Other times, I saw the ministry of a gift bring lasting reconciliation to broken relationships.

But I also began to see that I had good reason to doubt the truth of much of what went on. Too many "prophecies" just never panned out. "Words of knowledge" turned out to be anything but. "Miraculous" healings frequently lasted only until the meeting was over. As the pastor, I had to explain away these incongruities, without undermining charismatic doctrine. That wasn't easy.

But my pastor's role showed me problems that were much deeper than these, and more significant. I did a lot of counseling. When I began that ministry, I was rather dismayed at seeing the people who came to me for help. Many of them were the very folks who were at all the Bible studies, who shared their spiritual gifts in the afterglows, who took notes during the sermons, whose Bibles were extensively marked, who worked in the Sunday School, who sang on the worship team. They listened to Christian music, attended Christian seminars, and read every new Christian bestseller that hit the market.

But as they sat in my office, often in tears, every one of them would invariably ask the same question: "When does all this Bible study and spiritual exercise actually begin to *change* me? When does it start to affect me in the real world—in my marriage, with my kids, in my work? When does it start to give me victory over sins that have plagued me all my life—which, despite all my 'spirituality,' are just as strong as they have ever been? I thought I was tapping into the Holy Spirit's power here in this church. Why don't I feel Jesus deep in my heart? Where is this lasting peace and freedom He promises?"

The truth is, I could offer them no real answers. I was beginning to ask myself the very same questions! But since I was the pastor, and supposed to know the answers, I'd eventually reply with the best advice I could give: "Keep going to the Bible studies and afterglows, really focus on the sermons, keep reading your Bible and praying, use your spiritual gifts, stay involved in the church, keep listening to Christian music, and set your mind on things above."

At that point, they would usually give me a little nod of the head, and a weak, silent smile. Then off into their less-than-satisfying lives they would return, to do the same old things, with the same old results. Or perhaps they headed off to the Christian bookstore, hoping that *this* time, a new Christian author had at last hit on the magical principle they desperately needed to salvage their spiritual lives.

The End of the Line

Charismatic life, I had hoped, would establish my heart in biblical truth and thus restore me to that simple, childlike communion with Christ that I'd been trying to rediscover for over twenty years. Yet despite my herculean efforts and my devotion to Christ, this was not happening for me. Nor was it happening for those who were depending on me to help them achieve it.

Why?

I did not know the answer. The whole matter was very confusing to me. After all, charismatic practices thrilled me. There was a breadth and depth of energy that came with this life. Even when it was quiet in an afterglow, I could still feel the tingling in the atmosphere around me, and a vibrant anticipation within. The powerful allure of these inward stirrings had drawn me to the charismatic world. I had been sure these were the signs of God's Presence in my soul. How, then, could I still be feeling so empty?

On top of that, there were doctrinal struggles. My nondenominational congregation was showing some definite differences of opinion regarding issues like eternal security and the actual timeframe of the rapture. Serious contentions were arising, and I needed to set people straight on the truth. But after years of endless study, I found myself making fewer and fewer definitive statements about doctrine. I was becoming increasingly disillusioned by the fact that in the Protestant world, so many devout people could interpret the Scriptures in so many different ways. It seemed to me that truth, for a Protestant Christian, is whatever you *interpret* it to be. If that's so, then Christian "truth" isn't truth at all—at least not in any biblical sense of the word. I simply couldn't accept that. The whole business left me in a doctrinal quandary.

Eventually, my inability to help either myself or anyone else deal with these issues overwhelmed me. I left the ministry. For years, I moved from church to church, hoping someone else had found the elusive answers. There were occasional signs of life in places; but all too soon, these would fizzle out.

One night, after a very disillusioning experience at the church I was attending, I was unable to sleep. In the middle of that warm and moonless summer night, I walked outside beneath the stars. I cried out in tears to God, "Where are You? I am so lost."

In a heartbeat, Christ was with me—just like on that day when I was nine. His Presence was as large within my soul as the heavens that shone above me. But what I later realized most vividly about that moment was that this first-love awareness of His Presence was a world removed from my charismatic sense of "being in the Spirit." There were no feelings of elated exuberance. In truth, I couldn't describe His Presence as a feeling at all. It was more like a universe of living silence. It was not electric or exhilarating. Rather, it was overwhelming peace. It did not make me want to clap, shout, or swoon. Instead, it made me long for perfect stillness.

There in that night, I briefly touched what St. Paul refers to as the "peace of God, which surpasses all understanding" (Philippians 4:7). Oh, how I had forgotten. In all those moments in my life when I had been most aware of the Person of Jesus, it was *peace* that I'd felt. It was peace I'd felt when I thought that snakebite might kill me, when my grandfather died, and on that life-changing Saturday morning. Now here Jesus was again, revealing Himself to me in quiet love and peace that transcended both thought and emotion.

A New Journey Begins

But once again, my awareness of His glorious Presence faded. I was left to prayerfully take stock of the previous forty years of my life. I'd traveled many different denominational paths. Where had it brought me? On the positive side, my Protestant heritage had inspired in me the desire to seek out the truth, instilling in me a devotion for the Holy Scriptures. Along my way, there were many teachers, writers, and preachers who encouraged me to seek a deeper, living experience with Christ.

Yet I found myself at forty years of age with neither the assurance that my doctrine represented truth, nor the abiding awareness of the living Christ that I so earnestly craved. To me, Protestant faith had shown itself to be a great dream that cannot find its fulfillment, a deep question that cannot answer itself, an eternal thirst dwelling in a land of shallow wells.

So what was the problem? *Maybe,* I thought, *it's just me.* Perhaps what I was looking for was not to be found. Maybe truth is just something you aim at, but aren't ever supposed to find. In fact, I'd had a number of well-meaning friends tell me that I was just too concerned about truth. I shouldn't worry about doctrine, they told me. I should just trust in Jesus.

This, by the way, is a very fashionable idea among people who have become altogether disillusioned with their churches. It also spoke to that memory in my soul of the Jesus I knew before I was introduced to theology. But while I was sure that God wanted me to recover my childhood faith in Him, I was certain that He also wanted me to have a grown-up understanding of Him. After all, St. Paul tells us that we must grow from spiritual childhood to spiritual adulthood (1 Corinthians 13:11). What's more, I knew it was Christ Himself who had left me with that haunting question—*Is what you believe the Truth?*—so many years before.

So I realized that "Don't worry about doctrine; simply trust in Jesus" is overly simplistic advice. It doesn't tell the whole story. For before someone can follow such a course in any meaningful way, he first must have dealt with at least *one* question of doctrine: "*Who* is the Jesus I trust? Is He the Jesus whom many declare, who foreordains who's going to Heaven and who's not, in an eternal, irrevocable decision of His sovereign will? Is He, rather, the Jesus that others proclaim, who makes being saved and staying saved a free choice of an individual's own will? Or is He some other Christ, whose heart, will, and attitude toward His human creatures is different still?"

No, the question *What is the truth?* is unavoidable. For unless I'm sure I know the truth about Christ, how do I know that my Christian faith isn't just an illusion? The human mind and emotions are powerful things. It's absolutely possible to create a mental picture of someone and have an intense relationship with him or her, even though he or she isn't *real*. Think about the imaginary friends many of us have as children. If I'm not absolutely certain that I know the truth about who Christ is, my Christian life could simply be a love affair with an imaginary Friend.

Oh, I may have created my image of Him through intense study of the Scriptures. But He could be just a mistaken interpretation, an erroneous doctrine, to which I respond with great love and passion. So I could not sidestep issues of truth merely by saying, "I just trust in Jesus."

The more reasonable answer, it had seemed to me, was that my proud and sinful heart just kept me dissatisfied and blind to the truth. Maybe I was an unteachable disciple who didn't know how to be happy in Christ, and never would. Yes, that was the greater probability. There under the stars, I realized *that* was the depressing answer I had been embracing for some time.

But after that night, other disheartened people started visiting me. They came because they were struggling with the same issues.

Their proposed solution was to get me to start a home fellowship. I refused. I just couldn't imagine how becoming another little shard of the already pulverized vessel called Protestantism could possibly help any of us.

Nevertheless, that experience awakened me from my blue funk. Obviously, the problem wasn't just mine. Many shared my disillusionment. So I had to look deeper and more carefully for the answer. If the problem wasn't just with me, what else could it be?

I began prayerfully to analyze my situation. In my lifelong search for truth, I had traveled from one Protestant theology to another. When one path proved disappointing, I simply assumed that I needed to take up a different one. But none of the roads I'd followed had fulfilled my spiritual longings.

Then an incredibly stunning thought struck me: What if the problem with each of these denominations were not to be found in its *own distinctive* teachings? What if they all had failed me due to the very thing they hold in common—the fact that they are all *Protestant*?

I had spent a lifetime uncovering the faulty foundations of various denominations. But what if the footings of *Protestantism itself* were defective? This for me was a profound thought. It would explain why I still could not say, "This is the truth. Here is where I can truly live in the Presence of Christ."

But how would I go about investigating that possibility? To start with, I had to identify those characteristics that are shared by all Protestant denominations (or at least, by those that would consider themselves Bible-centered). I came up with three. Interestingly, it appears to me that even those contemporary Bible-believing churches that try to avoid defining labels like "Protestant" have these same traits. Here's what I observed:

(1) All these groups demonstrate a willingness to invent the church. By that I mean that they are all prepared to say, "Ours is the correct doctrine and way of worship, as opposed to what other groups say." Were this not the case, there would be just *one* Bible-believing Protestant denomination.

(2) It is an interesting paradox that the very mechanism that allows each Bible-centered group to make its claim of *uniqueness* happens to be a doctrine that is fundamental to *all* of them—*sola scriptura*. This is the belief that truth is determined by the Scriptures alone, without help from Church history. The reason we end up with thousands of Protestant denominations and nondenominations is because each has a different guiding principle for handling *sola scriptura*. Thus they can attain conflicting "biblical truths."

(3) Truth is a rational thing. It is discovered and evaluated by applying one's faculty of understanding to the Scriptures. Experience is considered an untrustworthy teacher. Any act or belief that one claims as Christian must square with the teachings of the Bible. To make such judgments requires careful reasoning and knowledge of biblical information and principles of biblical interpretation.

The Stage Is Set

With these points identified, I realized the task that lay before me was much the same as the one I had shouldered when I left Seventh-Day Adventism years before. But the question *Is it the truth?* was one I would now apply not just to some single *denomination*, but to the entire *system* of Protestant belief. I did not look forward to that at all. The potential results were not something I liked to ponder. Protestantism was the only Christianity I knew. Were I to find it faulty in its very foundations, where would I go?

Given the experiences of my life, I could not dispute the reality of the Person of Jesus Christ. Were I to give up on Protestantism, the only alternative I could envision was Roman Catholicism. But I could not see myself ever accepting the doctrines of papal supremacy and papal infallibility.

Thus it was with a grave and sober spirit that I began an investigation that would forever change my life.

⇢ 3 ⇠

Gods of the Scriptures

One day, I stood in a large, interdenominational Protestant gathering. We were singing the chorus, "In our hearts, we're undivided." On my left was a friend who is a firm advocate of "once saved, always saved." On my right was a friend who is just as adamant in his belief that salvation is something one can choose to lose. Nevertheless, both were caught up in the song's warm declaration of unity. It testified to the fact that, despite their differences, these brothers were united in the undivided, invisible Body of Christ.

For most of my life, I would have joined sincerely in that confident spirit of oneness. But this event occurred during that time when I was questioning the basic tenets of my Protestant belief system. As I said at the end of the last chapter, I wanted to discover what this phenomenon of denominationalism—this practice of inventing the church over and over again—revealed about the nature of my Protestant faith. So instead of singing exuberantly, I stood there pondering: *How can people who are so clearly divided in their beliefs possibly claim to be "one"?*

Finding a Flaw

Let me go back to the two friends I've just mentioned. They hold opposing viewpoints regarding the nature of salvation. Were you to ask either of them, "Whose theology is correct here—yours, or the other fellow's?" the answer would be, "Mine, of course." No other answer could be given. After all, it is absolutely impossible for a person to place real trust in a doctrine that he believes to be false, or even just possibly true. When it comes to matters of my Christian faith, saying "I believe this" is clearly the same thing as saying, "This is the truth."

So how do people with different versions of the truth joyously declare, "In our hearts we're undivided"? The most common answer to that question is: *When it comes to the crucial, defining issues of faith and salvation, all Protestants are really in agreement.* Now, for the very first time in my life, I asked myself, *Okay, what exactly* are *those points on which we are all agreed, regardless of our denominational allegiances?*

My first response to that question was immediate. I'd read the First Epistle of St. John many times. The Apostle teaches that to be recognized as a true follower of Christ, one must profess that Jesus is the incarnate Son of God: "By this you know the Spirit of God: Every spirit that confesses that Jesus Christ has come in the flesh is of God" (1 John 4:2). All Bible-believing Protestants would endorse that confession. This, I thought, is the glad common ground. Here is where a Protestant can lay aside his concerns over denominationalism and start to sing, "In our hearts, we're undivided," with deep and honest conviction.

Then I realized something. The fact that people jointly claim "Jesus is the Son of God come in the flesh" is *not* the true test of their unity. To be one in their confession, they must *mean the same thing* by their words. But by now, it was becoming clear to me that people within the Protestant realm mean very different things when they profess this most fundamental doctrine of Christianity. What specific part of this statement generates the variations in meaning? The most important word of all—*God.*

Am I a Christian?
You see, many Protestants mean by this confession that Jesus is the Son of that God who, in His mercy and grace, extends the gift of salvation to anyone who would choose to receive it. Not that He forces it upon anyone. No, He is the God who creates humans as free moral agents and respects each one's right to freely accept or deny His incomparable gift. So great is this God's respect for the personal sovereignty of His human creatures that He will even allow one who has already taken the gift to later reject it.

Other Protestants lean toward this meaning: Jesus is the Son of that God who exerts His sovereignty over every aspect of creation. This includes the predetermination of who will and who will not be redeemed. Human free will and human choice have no influence in the matter. Salvation is granted to those God elects. For people so chosen, salvation is an irrevocable reality. "Once saved, always saved" is the maxim. Damnation is the equally irrevocable fate of those whom He does not elect for redemption.

Other Protestants find neither of these views acceptable, and form still different pictures of God. Whatever the understanding of God I happen to hold, it is obvious that how He relates to His human creatures will affect the entire spectrum of my doctrine. It will color the meaning of every claim I make about God. So, whether it's "God is love," or "We are saved by grace through faith in Jesus Christ," or whatever the slogan they may mutually invoke, different Protestants mean distinctly different things by it.

For instance, when I say, "Jesus is Lord," do I mean the Lord who reveres human free will, or the Lord who has no room for free will in His Kingdom? After all, they can't both be the same God. When I say, "I'm saved by grace," am I talking about a salvation and a grace that extends to every human creature? Or am I referring to a salvation and a grace that God will grant only to some restricted, foreordained group?

I remember shuddering inside as for the first time in my life I really opened my eyes to the implications here. I happened to be someone who held to what is known among Protestants as an Arminian view of salvation—that God offers salvation to all, and that one who freely chooses to be saved can later freely choose to reject that salvation. For my whole Protestant life, I had assumed that I was nevertheless essentially of one faith with my Calvinist brethren, who believe that God chooses an elect group to be saved, and that when you're saved, you're always saved. I'd explained away this clear disparity in our viewpoints by telling myself, *We serve the same God. We just have different interpretations of Him.*

It is certainly true that the infinite God can reveal Himself to people in uniquely personal ways. St. Paul's relationship to God, for instance, appears very different from King David's. The picture of

Christ that is painted by St. John in his Gospel is readily distinguished from the one revealed by St. Matthew.

But now I saw that the differences between my Calvinist brethren and me (actually, between me and *anyone* with a different understanding of salvation) could not be dismissed as this sort of acceptable "personal" variation. God cannot *contradict* Himself. With Him, Scripture tells us, "there is no variation or shadow of turning" (James 1:17).

For the first time in my life, I saw that my understanding of God is not just different from that of my Calvinist brethren; it is contrary to it. Obviously, it is impossible for one and the same God to make free will the key to salvation's door, *and at the same time* eliminate free will from any real role in redemption. It is impossible for one and the same God to declare a man's salvation irrevocable, and at the same time proclaim it entirely revocable.

I realized that if God could act in such antithetical ways, I would be in the same poor boat as the Athenians with whom St. Paul debated on Mars' Hill (Acts 17). I would be worshiping an unintelligible, unknowable God. For what could I ever really know about the true nature of a God who is exactly who I believe Him to be, and at the same time, is exactly who I believe Him *not* to be? This means He could be absolutely anything—a truth-teller, and at the very same time, a heinous liar. The whole story of salvation could turn out to be just a cruel joke.

The simple truth that was being revealed to me was this: The God I worship *is a different God* from the one that Protestants who are not of my persuasion (Calvinist or otherwise) worship! The *same* God cannot have two, or three, or a hundred contradictory wills when it comes to his human creatures. He is One God, eternally unchanging, existing in three Persons: Father, Son, and Holy Spirit. That is one tenet of faith on which most Bible-believing Christians seem to agree.

That God is One, taken together with the fact that I worship a different God from other Protestants, left me with this incredibly unnerving insight: *If God is not who I believe Him to be, then I have no God.* If, in fact, it is my Calvinist friends who are right about

God, then the God I worship simply *does not exist.* There is no such thing as a God who allows men to freely choose, or lose, salvation. If that is the case, then I am not a Christian. I am not anything, for I worship a God who is false.

Of course, if I am the one who is right about God, then it is the Calvinists and others who are in the awful place of worshipping a false God. At last, I understood that the monumental question I needed to answer was not, "Am I right about my doctrine?" It was, rather, "Am I really a Christian?"

Truth Is Unimportant?

Denial is always the first reaction to a problem one does not want to face. I can assure you that I did not want to deal with the possibility that in my Protestant world, there might be many (including me) who were not really Christians. So the first thing I did was to try to come up with a method of explaining away the contradictions that were now starkly apparent to me. It seemed to me that I could avoid this problem if I could convince myself that either (1) it is not important that our beliefs about God are *actually* true, or (2) God *wants* His children to have different views of truth, or (3) *all* of these distinctive, contrary versions of truth are somehow equally *true.*

The first option was appealing. It was easy to chuckle and say to myself, *You're just playing theological games here. These issues aren't important. To be a Christian, all you have to do is love Jesus and live a good, moral, Christian life. God's not going to judge you on your theology.*

But I could not let myself off the hook that easily. I'd faced the fact that the God I was worshiping might not be real. So what does it matter if I live a good Christian life and call my Savior Jesus? If the God I love and worship is not real, I am no different from the fervent, kind-hearted heathen or the pious, morally upright pagan.

I knew scriptures that made it plain that just loving some "God" with all my heart and living a moral life will not impress God on Judgment Day. He expects commitment to the *true* Gospel. The Holy Apostle Paul tells us that we are saved by "belief in the *truth*"

(2 Thessalonians 2:13, italics mine). In his Epistle to the Galatians, he tells us that those who believe and preach a faith other than the true one are "accursed" (Galatians 1:9).

I thought about an idea I'd heard some Protestant thinkers present that really takes the pressure off when it comes to truth. That is, one can always fall back on the failsafe position, "Hey, even if I'm wrong when it comes to everything else about God, I trust that His Love is deep enough that He will overlook my errors in thinking and save me anyway."

I can understand how one could adopt this way of looking at things. When one envisions the broken and bleeding Lamb of God sacrificing Himself on the Cross, it seems like compelling evidence for such an all-encompassing, unqualified acceptance. Still, I had come face-to-face with the fact that different schools of Protestant thought have contrary ideas about what Jesus accomplished on that Cross. Does His Sacred Blood serve to cover every human who desires its cleansing, or does it save only an elect group? Obviously, my assumptions about God's designs for His human creatures affect even my definition of His Love and what His Love will lead Him to do.

So to believe that God's Love is such that He would save me regardless of what I believe about Him requires me to make some definite assumptions about the character and will of God. But if I am not absolutely certain that my understanding of His character and will are correct, then I have no basis whatsoever for trusting those assumptions. Unless I can say, "I know that I know the truth about God," my declarations of faith have no substance. They cannot establish me in a relationship with God, nor can I trust in their saving value. They are nothing more than wishful thinking.

Truth Is a Mosaic?
I had to believe that truth matters to God. He has spent millennia trying to reveal it to us fallen creatures. The Son of God has gone so far as to become one of us, to openly declare Himself the True God, in His truth separating Himself from all those false gods that humans love to embrace.

But this still left the door open for another way of sidestepping the question, *Who are the real Christians?* Perhaps, I speculated, it is somehow right and necessary that differing interpretations of God and of salvation should exist among Christians. Maybe this is the complex way by which God chooses to reveal His truth to the world.

I'd actually heard such an explanation set forth by some. The crux of their argument is that the current situation, in which different Christian groups have divergent views about the truth of God, is *exactly* the state of affairs that God wants. These teachers suggest God intends to bring all His children to a full knowledge of the truth at some time in the future. But for now, He has decided to scatter the truth like puzzle pieces throughout the various denominations of Protestantism. Each group gets a little bit of the truth. When Christ returns and establishes His Kingdom, all the denominations will come together, each bringing its little portion of the great puzzle. When these pieces are combined, a beautiful mosaic of truth will be revealed.

Why would God do things this way? One line of reasoning goes that God has allowed His children to hold a variety of incongruous beliefs specifically to prevent anyone from being able to claim, "I know the whole truth." If someone were actually to know the fullness of truth, according to this theory, that person would become haughty and proud, boasting, "I know the truth, but you just think you do!"

But wait! Simply knowing the truth does not automatically make a person conceited. I know, for instance, that the sun rises in the east. I know my car needs gasoline to run. None of this knowledge makes me swell with pride. That which is true is equally true for everyone. Believing it gives me no grounds for pride. If anything, this knowledge shows me that I am not in control, that there are things I can't change, that the world has a way of operating to which I have no choice but to submit (unless I am willing to embrace stupidity and its consequences).

The fact is, it appears to me that the modern Protestant situation—with its different versions of truth—creates religious conceit. For even when I tried to embrace the contradictory views of others as being somehow equally valid with my own, in my heart I was saying, "I'll accept you folks as brethren. But let's not forget that it's my beliefs that are the *true* ones!" I had to think that. Otherwise, I would have put myself in the schizophrenic position of believing that the things I had decided to be true either were actually false, or could be false. Were that the case, I couldn't really say I believed them. Considering all this, it became clear to me that if God wanted to prevent Christians from being puffed up over their religious beliefs, the best thing He could do would be to reveal the *same* truth to them all.

Whatever the other arguments that could be presented for this viewpoint, it seemed to me they could all be refuted by one simple observation. If each group or denomination has only a piece of the truth, then the rest of what each group believes must contain falsehood. To defend this point of view, I would have to hold that God either chooses, or is forced, to work out His plan for mankind by the use of lies. But St. Paul assures us that God "cannot lie" (Titus 1:2). That was enough to make me give up on the idea that God has decided, ostensibly for our own good, to hide the whole truth from us.

Relativism and "The Light That You Have"

Still desperate to find a way to view all believers as real Christians despite their contradictory concepts of the truth, I turned to an oft-invoked axiom. It seems to be the defense most Protestants raise when asked to account for the legitimacy of their particular beliefs in the face of the wide variety of Protestant beliefs and practices. The maxim goes: *You don't have to be concerned that other people have a different understanding of the truth. You just have to be true to your own convictions. One's relationship with God is an entirely personal thing. Just live up to "the light that you have," to what you believe the truth to be. That's what God expects.*

Of course, if this is the way things work, it means every person's version of the truth is correct—or at least correct enough to establish him in a saving relationship with God. It would show the question *Who are the real Christians?* to be completely pointless, and let me breathe easy again. So I began to consider carefully the implications of this train of thought.

First of all, such thinking makes sincerity of conviction the key to salvation. But this idea presents enormous problems. For instance, believing that sincerity is all it takes to make my faith a saving Christian faith necessarily implies I can believe absolutely anything about God and still confidently call myself a Christian. I just have to be fervently committed to those beliefs.

For a Christian, this generates thoroughly unacceptable conclusions. If sincerity is all it takes to be saved, then any Buddhist, Taoist, Muslim, Hindu, or pagan who is sincere can make the same claim to salvation as a sincere Christian. That would negate both Jesus' declaration that "no one comes to the Father except through Me" (John 14:6), and St. Peter's assertion that Jesus is the only "name under heaven given among men by which we must be saved" (Acts 4:12). We can be at once sincere, and sincerely wrong!

Obviously, then, being a Christian requires more than just sincerity. This business of truth is difficult for anyone who endorses a "just be true to the light that you have" attitude. It forces a person into taking one of two possible views about truth. Neither of these views, however, seems consistent with Christian faith. Let me review.

The first possible notion is one we have already considered, that truth is unimportant to God. Would it be fine with Him if we struck every instance of the word "truth" from the Scriptures? No, it seems impossible to believe that the Father who is worshipped in *truth* (John 4:24), the Son who is the *truth* (John 14:6), and the Spirit of *truth* who leads us into all *truth* (John 16:13) really don't care that I believe the *truth*.

The alternative picture of truth would be to see every idea regarding God and salvation as being equally true. In this way of thinking, everyone will be all right in the end, as long as each responds sincerely to his particular image of the truth. Anyone familiar with philosophy recognizes this as the age-old concept called *relativism*. It is the idea that truth is ultimately a purely subjective matter. The things that I believe are true simply because I believe them to be true. The fact that someone else has a different view of the truth is really of no concern to me.

As a Protestant believer, and especially as a pastor, I'd spent half a lifetime combating the moral relativism that runs rampant in our society. In doing so, I constantly raised the banner of "absolute truth." But I recognized now that as a Protestant who wanted to believe I was of one faith with people whose understanding of God is contrary to mine, I had all my life unquestioningly embraced a spiritual relativism that was very much like the moral relativism I'd spoken out against.

After all, how can I think that an Arminian and a Calvinist can both have a valid relationship with the true God, unless Jesus Christ can be a different Person to different individuals? St. James is quite clear, however: in God there can be no such "variation or shadow of turning" (James 1:17). The Apostle Paul assures us there is only one God, one Lord, one faith, one hope (Ephesians 4:4–6). How can there be room in the Christian faith for spiritual relativism?

Moving Toward an Answer

Under the weight of that thought, I began to review my three-pronged attempt at avoiding the question, *Am I really a Christian?* Does it matter to God that we believe the truth? Yes, it does; after all, God wants us to be one with Him (John 17:21, 22), and He *is* Truth. Does God scatter kernels of truth around among the denominations of Protestantism, carefully tucking them among half-truths and mistaken ideas? No, God will not (by nature, cannot) obscure the truth with error.

Relativism, then, is clearly inconsistent with Christian faith. It cannot represent a Christian understanding of truth. Why? It's because ultimately, relativism is inconsistent with the very *nature* of truth itself.

I thought about things I know to be true: fire burns, wind blows, the tides ebb and flow. And I saw that what makes truth the truth is that it *cannot* be relative. It cannot be twisted or seen in different lights. A man's personal convictions about it are meaningless. His only choices are to yield to it, or to defy it. Thus, the truth about

God must be the most purely objective truth there is. Still, as much as I wanted to say "Amen" to that statement, I realized my attitudes and actions demonstrated a strong ambivalence toward it.

An article I read back when I was struggling with these issues made that fact very clear to me. One Protestant writer was accusing another of being subjective in his doctrine. Now, I had to wonder: *Isn't that just a monumental case of the pot calling the kettle black?* The only way I could be rationally consistent in making such a statement is if I were the kind of Protestant who's willing to say, "My doctrine is the absolute truth, and Protestants who don't believe like me are heretics." But if I'm a Protestant who wants to think that people with contrary opinions about God are still united in their faith anyway, then I must believe doctrinal subjectivity and relativism are perfectly natural and acceptable.

Of course, I knew what my retort would be if someone were to charge *me* with being a relativist. I'd explain, "My doctrines are not based upon arbitrary, egocentric whims of fancy. My doctrines are to be found in the very concrete, objective words of the Bible. I stand on the Scriptures alone, avoiding all subjective 'doctrines of men.'"

Sola Scriptura:
The Heart of the Matter

I had held to *sola scriptura* all my life. This was a doctrine I was prepared to defend to the death. But I was trying to get to the truth now, and no stone could be left unturned. This problem of subjectivity seemed to me to be a huge issue. In fact, it was beginning to look to me as if, despite the way my Protestant brethren and I decried it, *Protestantism might be the greatest proponent of pure, subjective relativism that the world has ever known.* So I needed to ask, *Does sola scriptura rescue my faith from relativism and establish it on the rock of objective truth?*

During the course of my life, I had been involved with many denominations. Key elements of their theologies differed greatly. But, as I noted in Chapter 2, the one thing those churches all had in common was their insistence that their doctrines were grounded in *sola scriptura*—in "the Scriptures alone."

Bible-believing Protestants are absolutely right in their belief that the Scriptures are the repository of Christian truth. The Scriptures are inspired by the Holy Spirit. We receive the Bible as the Word of God. The strange paradox is that this doctrine of *sola scriptura* on which Protestantism was founded five hundred years ago is the very doctrine that splinters Protestantism into thousands of factions. How can this be?

While with the historic Church I believe without question that the Holy Scriptures are God-breathed by the Holy Spirit, I have come to the very difficult conclusion that *sola scriptura* is an utterly subjective doctrine. The Scriptures *alone* can never show us what the objective truth about God is. The amazing thing is, any Bible-believing Protestant who takes a second to examine how he approaches the Scriptures will find that he already knows that.

Let me explain. As I was working through this issue, I was reminded of a Sunday afternoon potluck I'd attended. Two cousins were good-naturedly going at it over the doctrine of salvation. Predictably, one believes in eternal security, one does not.

I listened as these two debaters, both of whom profess *sola scriptura*, skillfully and methodically made their cases. They were well read and provided corroborating evidence from famous teachers, preachers, and theologians. At the end of their debate, the two of them looked at me (I was their pastor at the time) and asked, "So, who wins?"

Just to avoid starting the whole row over again, I heaved a sigh and said, "Why doesn't one of you guys just point me to the scripture verse that plainly tells me which one of you is right?" Do you know what happened? Everybody in the room laughed! Then one of the guys chuckled, "Yeah, right—like it should be so easy!"

I found myself thinking, *It seems like it ought to be that easy. Why isn't it?* I realize today it's because the Scriptures, while providing the raw material for many diverse interpretations, do not give us a clear, unquestionable, uncontroversial means of deciding *which* of those interpretations is correct. If they did, all intelligent, Bible-believing Protestants would be precisely united in their doctrine. Doctrinal uniformity would be a piece of cake! But taken by themselves, the Scriptures cannot reveal to us the objective truth about God. Why? It's because they were never meant to stand by themselves!

And as I said, all Protestants already know this. When they go to church, they never hear the pastor just read the Scriptures aloud for forty minutes. He spends most of his time explaining what they mean. Why? The reason is that to teach us, to influence us, to reveal God to us, the Scriptures must be *interpreted*. That is why we pray that the one who preaches is "rightly dividing the word of truth" (2 Timothy 2:15). So what's important to a Protestant believer is not just "the Scriptures alone." What he actually puts his faith and trust in is his *interpretation* of "the Scriptures alone."

Now, the fact that the Scriptures must be interpreted is not in itself a problem. The Scriptures are words, and all words must be interpreted to be understood. I have to interpret the newspaper I read in the morning, the questions my students ask me in class, and the grocery list Alice sends with me to the store.

But understanding that it's my interpretations of the Scriptures that form my beliefs is a very important insight—especially for someone trying to answer the question, *Is what I believe the truth?* For the answer to *that* question will come when I can answer this one: *Are my interpretations of the Scriptures correct?* If the answer is *Yes*, then I can rest assured that I know the truth about God.

Subjective Evidence

So next, I excitedly set about trying to resolve that question. To what irrefutable evidence could I point as the basis for unqualified confidence in my interpretations of the Word of God? Much to my dismay, it didn't take long for me to realize it was impossible to provide any.

Let me illustrate the problem this way. In the course of my life's spiritual journey, I had studied, embraced, and finally rejected elements of several different theologies: Seventh-Day Adventist, fundamentalist, and charismatic. Proponents of each of these often-contradictory schools of thought would claim their theology to be based upon "the Scriptures alone." Facing this question about interpretations, it finally struck me that all of them—the Seventh-Day Adventist, the fundamentalist, the Pentecostal—are absolutely justified in making the claim that their theologies *are* based on the Bible!

What I mean is, I could make an irrefutable scriptural argument for almost any doctrine within these three different theologies. For instance, if I choose the right verses, I can make a thoroughly convincing argument from the Bible that the Seventh-Day Adventist is correct: we should all be worshiping on Saturday. But I can also present an airtight case from the Scriptures that would prove Christians are in no way required to observe the ancient Sabbath as their worship day. Which of these two arguments a listener would buy would not depend upon the Scriptures alone. It would come down to which interpretation he was willing to accept.

Different Protestant theologies use the same Scriptures. So clearly, it is their different methods of interpretation that make each system unique. The reason people end up with different methods of interpreting the Bible is that they approach the process with different *assumptions*. Unavoidably, we look at the Scriptures through different interpretive grids.

For instance, when it comes to the Sabbath, a Seventh-Day Adventist presupposes that every command of God stands unaltered forever. A Sabbath that God once ordained to be honored as the high day of holy worship must forever, even into eternity, be observed. The Adventist bases this assumption upon passages like the Ten Commandments (Exodus 20:8–11) and Isaiah 66:22, 23, which speaks of the Sabbath being observed in the future "new earth." What really makes him an Adventist and not, say, a Baptist, is the fact that he judges these particular passages to be the most weighty and significant when it comes to Sabbath questions. He thus interprets all other passages in accordance with that judgment—even those that say there is no longer any compulsion for Sabbath worship (like Colossians 2:16).

Those who would not accept seventh-day Sabbath worship as binding on Christians have different presuppositions. They start from the position presented in Colossians 2:16, giving it the greatest interpretive weight. The Sabbath, they say, as part of the Law, is a shadow of Christ. When one receives Christ, he goes beyond the shadow, beyond the Law, and can no longer be judged with regard to the day he keeps as a day of worship. All other scriptural references are understood in the light of the Incarnation of the Son of God. This includes the passage in Genesis 2, where God hallows and sanctifies the Sabbath long before the Sabbath command appears in the Law.

The huge question that faced me now was, *How would I go about objectively determining whose assumptions are the correct ones— about this issue or any other?* There is no way to conclusively determine the answer solely from the Scriptures. For the Scriptures themselves do not tell us which of its passages should be given greater interpretive weight over others.

Now, dedicated proponents of every theology may insist the principles on which they base their method of interpretation are to be found in the Scriptures. They point to various passages and say, "See, these texts show us how we are to interpret the Word of God correctly." But the problem remains the same. Adherents to different theologies point to different principles. Even where they agree on principles, they get different results! The Scriptures by themselves clearly do not teach us which scheme of interpretation, which doctrinal positions, we should embrace.

Then how do we make such judgments? When I got painfully honest with myself, I could see I made such judgments based upon whatever made the most sense to me. And what made the most sense to me was determined by some very subjective influences. My basic worldview, my personality, my family, my religious heritage, my society, my prejudices and biases, the persuasive power of the Bible teachers I had encountered—these decided how I interpreted the Scriptures.

My immediate reaction was to retort, *No! My interpretations are based on the guidance of the Holy Spirit. I come to the Scriptures with an honest heart, and trust the Holy Spirit to reveal the truth to me.* Problem is, my sincere, honest, truth-desiring brother who holds contradictory interpretations would say the very same thing!

Is the Holy Spirit directing both of us? If He is, then that leaves us with a most disconcerting picture of the Spirit of God. For the Spirit, whom Christ calls the Spirit of truth, is busily at work sabotaging the longings of the Son! On the night before His holy Passion, Christ prayed for his Apostles, and for all who would believe through them,

> that they all may be one, as You, Father, are in Me, and I in You; that they also may be one in Us, that the world may believe that You sent Me. And the glory which You gave Me I have given them, that they may be one just as We are one (John 17:21, 22).

One—just as He and His Father are one. This is what Jesus desires for His people. Now, do I believe the Godhead is infected with the sad disease of division? Do I believe the Father and the Son and the Holy Spirit, who fully share the one Divine Nature, cannot agree on the particulars when it comes to the truth? Of course not.

But to maintain that the contrary convictions of all Protestant believers are inspired by the Spirit of God is to accuse the Spirit of making sure the Church of Christ will be nothing like the Godhead in its oneness. So I was still left asking, *On what do I base my belief that my interpretations of the Scriptures represent the truth?*

The Sad Conclusion

I reviewed my meditative journey. I knew if I wanted a real first-love relationship with the real God, I had to be sure that I knew the truth about Him. The truth about God is settled, not open to debate. My Protestant faith rightly taught me this truth is to be found in the Scriptures. But the inspired Scriptures by themselves cannot tell me that my beliefs are true, since I must interpret them. Given the fact that other devoted Christians hold doctrines contrary to mine, I cannot really have confidence that the Holy Spirit guides *my* interpretations—unless I'm willing to believe either that the Holy Spirit wants to sow confusion in the world, or that *I'm* the only one to whom the Spirit reveals the truth, while He makes all those other dear people wallow in falsehood.

So on what did I base my understanding of God? On what was I banking my eternal destiny? As a Christian, in what did I place my faith? There is no way to describe the bitter, suffocating darkness that descended upon my heart and mind when the awful reality of my situation enveloped me. For at last I understood that the foundation of my Protestant faith was just *me*—sinful, erring, ignorant *me*.

It was clear my faith could not be founded on the Scriptures alone, and I had no objective grounds whatsoever for believing my personal interpretations of them were the work of the Holy Spirit. Obviously, my concept of truth rested ultimately upon my faith in myself—upon the completely unsupportable feeling that "since this is what makes sense to me, it's got to be correct." So when I asked the question, *How do I know that what I believe is the truth?* my

Protestant faith could give me but one answer: *Interpret the Scriptures as best you can, and just trust that you're right.*

But what if I were *wrong?* The Proverbs began to ring in my ears: "The way of a fool is right in his own eyes," and "There is a way that seems right to a man, / But its end is the way of death" (Proverbs 12:15; 14:12).

Here I stood, no longer blissfully self-assured in my doctrine, but rather wondering if it was I whom those verses were describing. Here, all the preaching in the world about "standing on the Scriptures" and "trusting to the leading of the Holy Spirit" could not hide the spiritual bankruptcy, the ironic emptiness, of my faith. For the only answer it could give me when I asked, *Am I a fool or not?* was simply, *Trust the convictions of your heart.*

All my life, I had longed to know God. I had traveled many Protestant roads searching for Him. I'd heard many different descriptions of what the True God is like. Now my heart went numb and cold. For I realized that after all that, the only answer my Protestant faith could give to the question, *Who is God?* was, *He is whoever you believe Him to be!*

At this point, I hung on the edge of complete despair. I was tempted to look upon life as a purposeless, directionless journey. Only two things upheld me. First and foremost were those cherished moments in my life when Jesus Christ had touched places in my soul that were fathomless. I knew He could be found. Secondly, the Scriptures gave me hope. Their blessed words told me that at least at one time in the Church, the truth was not obscured and made unknowable by conflicting subjective theologies:

> But we are bound to give thanks to God always for you, brethren beloved by the Lord, because God from the beginning chose you for salvation through sanctification by the Spirit and *belief in the truth,* to which He called you by our gospel, for the obtaining of the glory of our Lord Jesus Christ. Therefore, brethren, *stand fast and hold the traditions which you were taught, whether by word or our epistle* (2 Thessalonians 2:13–15, italics mine).

Once upon a time, there had been unconfused truth. There had been truth that all Christians believed and followed. The merciful God would not let me give up on finding it. But on that day, I finally knew it could not be found on the Protestant path where I had walked all my life. So after more than forty years, I sadly turned my back on the Christianity I had known. Into a night of uncertainty I plunged, seeking another way to Truth, another way to Love, another way to the Reality of the blessed Christ.

⇥ 5 ⇤

Faith and History

Against the subjectivity of my own heritage, Roman Catholicism presented a stark, objective contrast. Here is a Church ancient and seemingly unchanging. People within its walls do not run around all self-assured, ready to invent new doctrine or start new churches every time they don't like what the pastor teaches. These are not people who build their faith and hope upon unwavering confidence in themselves. In fact, as I began to associate with Catholic believers, I was quite surprised to find that many of them clearly see the problem with Protestant egocentrism.

For instance, I remember expressing to a Catholic friend the terrible guilt I'd felt once I had realized that I'd spent a lifetime trusting my salvation to my own self-assurance that *I* was the one who was right about God. To my amazement, he smiled knowingly. Then he said, "I understand. We Catholics have an old saying: 'Protestants believe that everyone is infallible, except the Pope!'"

I was now looking for something solid and outside of myself on which to ground my faith. With that goal, there were aspects of Catholicism that gave it strong appeal. Its age and universality made it an attractive foundation. Even its hierarchical and authoritative structure, which had once appalled me, now looked more comforting and right. Having rejected myself as the supreme judge of everything, I was now in a position to take seriously the clear New Testament teaching that Christ has established rulers in the Church, to whom the rest of us are to give obedience:

> Remember those who rule over you, who have spoken the word of God to you, whose faith follow, considering the outcome of their conduct. . . . Obey those who rule over you, and be submissive, for they watch out for your souls,

as those who must give account. Let them do so with joy and not with grief, for that would be unprofitable for you (Hebrews 13:7, 17).

But in the doctrines of papal universality and infallibility, my journey toward Roman Catholicism encountered a seemingly insurmountable obstacle. I was ready to accept the idea of rulership in the Church, but not the rulership of one man. For when I looked at history, this did not seem to be the sort of Church government that Peter and the rest of the Apostles had embraced.

For example, in the fifteenth chapter of Acts, we see the early Church leaders making a doctrinal decision for the Church at large. It was an important decision, but it was not based solely on Peter's judgment, or Paul's judgment, or James's judgment. Rather, it was the determination of a *council*. Furthermore, it was James, now Bishop of Jerusalem, who issued the verdict—not Peter. Even with my very limited understanding of Church history, I knew there had been other such councils in the early Church.

I did not just slam the doors on Roman Catholicism, though. I kept the doors open, constantly praying that the Lord would reveal to me the truth about His Church.

The Philosophical Road

One connection I made with Catholicism was to attend a Catholic university, where I pursued a graduate degree in philosophy. Theology had left me high and dry in my attempt to find truth. I wanted to see if philosophy—at least traditional, Western, God-centered philosophy—might help me rediscover an abiding sense of the Presence of Christ.

I was not to be disappointed. One of the most significant turning points in my lifetime search for truth occurred during my studies. No, I didn't learn some philosophical principle that suddenly made everything clear. Rather, in the course of my philosophical research, I discovered some historical facts that forever changed my life. The first of those facts had to do with a Protestant doctrine with which I'd always struggled: the Atonement.

All my evangelical life, I'd had a problem with one particular aspect of the way in which I was taught to present the gospel. Somewhere in the course of evangelizing an unbeliever, I was supposed to make the point that God demands that a penalty be paid for sin. His Holiness requires satisfaction for the great injury our human sinfulness has inflicted upon Him.

Of course, what we are to see as glorious in all this is the fact that God Himself mercifully paid the penalty He demanded, through the sacrifice of His Son. But this gave me pause. I was worried someone might ask, "Why does there have to be a penalty? Doesn't Jesus teach we are to forgive freely the wrongs done to us? In fact, aren't we told to take no more thought of them? Why does God expect us to do this, while He does not? Why does He have to have his 'pound of flesh' as a payment for wrongs done to Him, but forbids *us* to demand the same? If we come to Him asking pardon, why can't He Himself do what He commands us to do, and simply say, 'I forgive'?"

I had long searched for an answer. I contemplated issues like the balance between justice and mercy, and the infinite difference between my holiness and God's. Still, this picture of God always seemed to me contradictory to the way He reveals Himself in Christ.

Then while in graduate school, I learned something astounding. I discovered that the Protestant and Roman Catholic view of the Atonement, often called the "substitution" or "satisfaction" theory, didn't arrive on the scene until the very end of the eleventh century. That's when St. Anselm, a Roman Catholic philosopher and theologian, worked it out. Of course, that left me with the intriguing question, *What did the Church believe about the Atonement before then?*

One day, while searching a philosophical volume for information on a matter totally unrelated to the Atonement, I ran across an entry that gave me the answer to that question. It was so beautiful that my heart literally leapt within me. For its first thousand years, I read, the Christian Church did not teach that the sacrifice of Christ was an attempt to satisfy the honor of God. Instead, it taught that Jesus' death was the costly ransom paid voluntarily by the Son of

God to rescue the creatures He loves from the inescapable power of death. By Christ's sacrifice, believers are freed from death's demands and from all accusations of the devil.

Excitedly, I hurried to the library and began to look at the early Church writings the commentary cited. Previously, I had not even known these works existed. But it was perfectly evident from them that this was indeed what the Church originally taught about the Atonement.

Here, I thought, is a doctrine that is easily understood. More importantly, here is a view of the Atonement that lights the night of the human soul with sublime mercy. It reveals a truly redeeming God, not One who is angered by smudges to His honor and requires a payoff. No, His loving, self-sacrificing work is to rescue us for Himself from the power of sin, Satan, and death, not from His own displeasure with us. What the Son of God truly wants as a result is achieved: the just reconciliation of His creation to Himself.

I wept for joy. And then for pain. For though I was elated by this clearer vision of His mercy, I was struck hard by a more profound sense that Jesus' suffering was truly all because of me. The plan of salvation does not revolve around so lofty a goal as the restoration of God's honor. No, it's just about miserable me—miserable *us*—in desperate need of a Savior, and One who came willingly and uncommanded, in a cascade of humility, to save us.

How vividly I recall that life-changing moment. As I sat there cross-legged on the floor between two great shelves of books, open volumes of early Christian writings scattered all around me, a new and glorious day dawned upon me. Its bright sun began to cast its rays on me the minute I asked myself the question, *I wonder what else was different in the Church during those first thousand years of its existence?* Over the coming months, the discoveries began to flow like a waterfall of truth.

I must admit most of the things I learned about that first-millennium Church shook my modern Protestant roots. Even the earliest Christian writings revealed to me a Church that definitely looked very "Catholic." I'd always been told these doctrines and practices began to show up in later centuries. But here's a list of things I learned about the early Church from the writings of Christian leaders who were either converted in the time of the Apostles, or lived in the hundred years or so after the death of the longest surviving Apostle, St. John:

(1) From Pentecost on, the worship of the Church was liturgical, not spontaneous or free-form. As a Protestant, I'd always assumed primitive Church worship must have looked pretty much like a charismatic home fellowship. But that notion is erroneous. Even the Book of Acts shows it to be wrong.[1]

(2) Early Church worship centered on the Eucharist or Communion. Writings from the late first century showed me that to those early believers, the bread and wine were not just symbols; they were, albeit in a mystical way, the actual Body and Blood of Christ. In fact, one of the earliest heresies in the Church was the teaching that the bread and wine were not the real Body and Blood of the Lord.[2]

(3) The early Church honored departed saints as members of the Church who are alive and worshiping in heaven.[3]

(4) Infant baptism was the standard practice in the Church and was recognized as a doctrine "received from the Apostles."[4]

Just as enlightening as these writings were my encounters with the men who wrote them. Most of these great Christian leaders—like St. Ignatius, St. Polycarp, St. Justin, St. Irenaeus, St. John Chrysostom, St. Basil, St. Gregory, St. John of Damascus, and St. Maximos the Confessor—had been entirely unknown to me. But their lives revealed to me holy men of a spiritual caliber that could not be matched by even the greatest spiritual heroes of modern times. In their writings, I saw revealed a Church vitally connected to the Apostles, full of godly power and divine love, which spiritually bore almost no resemblance to the Protestant tradition in which I had been raised. In short, I saw a Church where leaders and laymen alike were consumed with the love of Christ. To them, Jesus Christ was not a collection of doctrines, but a living Person whose abiding Presence was more real to them than anything else in the world.

History, Not Theology

Obviously, I was smitten with the beauty of that first-millennium Church. My heart felt more alive and open to the Presence of Christ than it had felt in thirty years. But my journey had taught me that I can be a most self-deceiving person. In the past I had heartily embraced things that I had later determined to be false. No, just the fact that I was *moved* by the teachings and practices of the early Church was no guarantee that its doctrine and worship embodied the truth of Christ.

So, how could I be sure they did? I'd fled Protestantism because I'd rejected the idea that real truth could be grasped through subjective interpretation of the Scriptures. How could I know that the teachings of the first-millennium Church weren't just the wacky, subjective interpretations of ancient heretics? As a Protestant, that's what I had always believed them to be. What could I point to as evidence for trusting that this Church worshiped in truth?

One day, as I was thinking about all this, the Scripture that had sustained me in my journey out of Protestantism came to mind:

> But we are bound to give thanks to God always for you, brethren beloved by the Lord, because God from the beginning chose you for salvation through sanctification by the Spirit and belief *in the truth*, to which He called you by our gospel, for the obtaining of the glory of our Lord Jesus Christ. Therefore, brethren, *stand fast and hold the traditions which you were taught, whether by word or our epistle* (2 Thessalonians 2:13–15, italics mine).

I remember just how hard it hit me. All my life, I had searched for truth in a theological way. I'd been taught to study the Scriptures, apply a system of interpretation to them, and call what I gleaned from my personal study "the truth." Now, I saw that the truth of Christ, the truth of His Church, was never meant to be conveyed and sustained in that way! St. Paul *did not* call the Church to theologize. He did not admonish his children to kick around various doctrines and adopt the ones that seemed most reasonable to them. Rather, he told the believers at Thessalonica to stand fast and hold to the traditions that they had been taught—those that came through epistles, and the many that came directly from the mouths of the Apostles.

Please understand. For a modern Christian who wants to answer the question, *How do I know that what I believe is the truth?* these words of St. Paul are among the most important ever recorded. For he was clearly telling the early Christians that they had *just one way* of knowing that they were living in the truth. To have that assurance, they had to be able to say, *"We believe and do those things that the Church of Christ has believed and done from the beginning— from the Day of Pentecost!"*

What a powerful revelation this was for me. I saw it was possible for me to be free from subjectivity. I just had to accept the fact that Christian truth is to be found within the historic Church itself, not in the subjective interpretations of Protestant theology.

Rapidly, the teachings of Christ and His Apostles with regard to truth began to converge in my mind. Jesus made a significant and straightforward promise regarding truth in this pledge to His Apostles: "When He, the Spirit of truth, has come, He will guide you into *all* truth" (John 16:13, italics mine). He didn't say that the Spirit would lead the Apostles into *part* of the truth, or into the *beginnings* of the truth, but into truth in its entirety. At Pentecost, the Spirit came. If we are to believe Christ's promise, we must accept that within the course of their lives and ministries, the Apostles together were led to a full understanding of Christ—or at least, to the fullness of the Faith—by the Holy Spirit.

The Apostles, St. Paul tells us, formed the "foundation" of the Church of Christ (Ephesians 2:20). So from the Apostles, truth spread to every believer. Thus, St. Paul confidently declares that the Church itself is the "pillar and ground of the truth" (1 Timothy 3:15).

For the first time in my life, I think, I was able to really *hear* that scripture. All my life, I had held the Scriptures to be "the pillar and ground of the truth." But St. Paul is plain in his language: to find the foundation of Christian truth, we must look to a living vessel, the Body of Christ. The Church is not a Book, even though a sacred

Book tells us its story. Rather, the Church is a living reality. To know what is the truth, therefore, does not first require theological interpretation of the Book. Rather, it simply takes looking at the actual beliefs, practices, and experiences of the Church of which Christ is the Head, which the Apostles served, lived out on the pages of history.

Of course, the problem I faced was that written on those pages of the Church's early history were doctrines and worship practices that the Reformation had rejected. It declared them to be "unscriptural." I had raised that cry against them myself. I had pointed at many of those doctrines and proclaimed them the "doctrines of men."

Now, though, I could see things differently. I realized that, when it came right down to it, it was my Protestant beliefs that were the real doctrines of men! After all, they were doctrines that other *men* and myself had subjectively determined for ourselves to be right, even while many other sincere Christian men proclaimed them wrong. Clearly, if the unchanging, unerring God were the true source of our doctrine, there would be no such disagreement. There can be no such thing as conflicting "doctrines of God." So when I had squabbled with other Protestant believers over our differing doctrinal interpretations, what else could we possibly have been arguing, except competing doctrines of men?

One of the things I quickly learned was that, just like Bible-believing Protestants, the Christians of that early "Catholic-looking" Church held the Scriptures to be the bulwark of their Christian faith. It's just that they saw those beliefs and practices at which a Protestant typically balks to be perfectly consistent with the teachings of the New Testament.

I finally realized my old accusations that these doctrines were unscriptural did not automatically make them false. But still the question remained, *Are they true?* In answering that question, I came to a revelation about the nature of truth that changed my life forever.

→ 6 ←

Truth Is a Promise

As I struggled with the possibility that doctrines I'd rejected all my life might actually be true, I was reminded of another beautiful vow that Jesus had made regarding His Church. He declares, "The gates of Hades shall not prevail against it" (Matthew 16:18). At no point, Jesus assures us, will the powers of hell and the devil be able to undermine this pillar of truth.

At that point, I started pulling together all the New Testament teachings I could find regarding truth. Jesus promised that the Church He founded upon His Apostles would know the truth. In that truth the Church would be forever established. It would stand unshakable against all assaults by Satan, the father of lies.

Suddenly, I had a novel thought: *What if I simply take Jesus at His word? What if I actually accept His promises to His Church as true, and believe that He has given His Church the truth and has kept that truth unassailable from the enemy?*

First of all, I perceived this would mean that those teachings and practices I had previously dismissed as "Catholic" and "unscriptural" might actually be Spirit-inspired. The Faith as it was understood and practiced everywhere by millions of believers for at least a millennium would embody the truth Christ gave to the Apostles—if I believed that Jesus had the power to live up to His promises.

Secondly, accepting the promises of Christ would at last give me that divinely objective, outside-of-myself measure of faith for which I was seeking. No longer would I be stuck with "truth" that amounted to nothing more than my personal interpretations of the Scriptures. I didn't have to merely trust myself anymore. I could trust Christ, and what He said about the Church, instead of looking to Martin Luther, or John Calvin, or myself. If I believed Christ's promise never to let His Church fall into the hands of the enemy, then I could trust that the Faith practiced always and everywhere by His undivided Church represented the truth about who God is and about how He desires to relate to His people.

An objective foundation for my Christian faith, plain as the light of day, one that doesn't require my personal interpretations—*that* was what accepting the promises of Christ would give me. Of course, I also realized that before, I simply had refused to believe His promises! As a Protestant, I firmly believed the Church of Christ had started going "to hell in a hand-basket" within a generation or two of its origin. As a Protestant, I was convinced Jesus was relatively helpless for fifteen hundred years or so against the evil designs of men who were the ordained successors of the Apostles, but who were actually out to destroy the Church of Christ—even though they were routinely martyred in His Name. As a Protestant, I believed Christ was either unwilling or powerless to do anything, as He watched millions of people who thought they were Christians live and die in falsehood. Not until the advent of Protestantism, I thought, did the Church of Christ become a force that could truly withstand the gates of Hades.

I remember the day I realized I had lived my whole life in this awful faithlessness. How could I have thought my Lord to be the most powerless God ever worshiped? I had believed Him able to save me, but utterly unable to preserve truth in His people for even a single generation. What an impotent and uncaring God my beliefs had proclaimed our Lord Jesus Christ to be! Falling to my knees, weeping bitterly in repentance for such ignorance, I begged Him to forgive me.

And in a breath, He was there in my soul, filling me with His loving Presence. For the first time in a long time, I heard His silent voice. He said, *Don't lose heart now, Matthew. You are not far from the Kingdom.* In my heart of hearts, and with every ounce of volition my soul could muster, I vowed to Him that I would be blind and faithless no longer.

Settling Questions
The first thing that adopting an historical view of truth did for me

was to eliminate doctrinal uncertainty from my life. For every major issue over which Protestants dispute, I found the early Church had clear answers. One of the first doctrinal questions I forever resolved was the one I mentioned in Chapter 4—the business of the Sabbath. In the light of the early Church's teaching, I found that neither the Seventh-Day Adventist nor the Sunday-worshipping Protestant has it quite right when it comes to the Sabbath.

Here's the truth, according to the early Church: Saturday is the Sabbath. The early Church recognized it as a holy day, in that it is the day that commemorates God's resting after the creation of the world. Also, the Church revered it as the day on which Christ descended into hell, shattering its gates and freeing mankind forever from the bonds of death.

But the early Church also understood that the act the Sabbath commemorates—the creation of the world—has been infinitely surpassed in the continuing work of God, the new creation, which St. John describes: "Now I saw a new heaven and a new earth, for the first heaven and the first earth had passed away" (Revelation 21:1). When does this new universe begin? On the day of Christ's glorious Resurrection. For on that day, God established the foundations of this new world, a world that includes eternal life for mankind. It was on the day of His Resurrection that Christ our God rose in the flesh, forever making possible our union with Him. By the power of His Resurrection, man is blessed by the indwelling of the Holy Spirit and may live in oneness with the Father under the earnest of those new heavens, in that new earth.

Now, the old creation was commemorated on the day of its *ending*—on Saturday. But the new creation will never pass away. Thus, it must be commemorated on the day of its wondrous beginning. And that day, the day on which God chose to raise Christ and gloriously change the universe forever, is not Saturday, but Sunday. The ancient Church often referred to Sunday as the "eighth day," the day that takes us beyond this awesome, but temporal and fading realm that the Sabbath remembers, into God's eternal day.[1]

The Church recognizes its first allegiance must belong to the new, everlasting Kingdom, not to the old. Thus, the faithful of Christ proclaimed Sunday as their day of highest worship. Saturday remained a day for spiritual meditation and reflection, a day to thoughtfully prepare for the celebration of Christ's Resurrection.

Whether it was the Sabbath, or the nature of salvation, or end-time events—whatever the issue—I found the early Church had specific teachings that remained from the start unaltered, century after century.

Where Is the New Testament Church?

I expressed earlier the major concern I had with Roman Catholicism. It was the whole issue of Church government. Specifically, it was the belief that one man has infallible authority over the Church of Christ. But I was at a point where I realized that unless I could find a Church that fully embodied early Church doctrine, Roman Catholicism was the closest I would come.

My study of Church history had not served to lessen my concerns about papal infallibility. In fact, it heightened them. For that study acquainted me with the seven great Ecumenical Councils of the Church, held from AD 325–787. These councils were gatherings called to address enormous doctrinal disputes. When major questions arose, the bishops of Christendom would meet together in some ancient city to answer them.

But the glorious thing is, these Councils never produced innovative doctrines. In answering the question, *What is the truth?* the great Councils were all guided by a single principle, once expressed simply and beautifully by St. Vincent of Lerins: The truth is "that faith which has been believed everywhere, always, by all."[2] When new and heretical ideas arose, the bishops reaffirmed and clarified that which had been believed by Christians everywhere and always, from the time of the Apostles. This explains how Christian belief and practice in, say, the tenth century, could in every important respect look just like Christian belief and practice in all the preceding centuries.

The stories of these Councils made me question papal authority, since every bishop had an equal voice in those meetings. While the patriarch of Rome was first in honor, each bishop cast one vote.

Yes, some bishops—particularly those of the great Christian centers of Jerusalem, Antioch, Rome, Alexandria, and Constantinople—commanded the greatest respect. After all, their high-profile positions often required them to be great champions of the Faith. They also stood a greater-than-average chance of dying for Christ. But when it came to Council decisions, while usually the local bishop presided, each bishop had the same voting power, whether he was from one of the great cities or from the smallest village in Christendom.

The obvious question was, of course, *When did the Pope of Rome claim greater power?* I found that out when my wife attended a presentation on the Eastern Orthodox Church. She told me the speaker that evening had discussed an event in Church history called the Great Schism. Now, I'd never heard of it—which wasn't a great surprise to me at that point. When I started studying the early Church, I learned quickly that, as a Protestant, I knew essentially nothing about events in Christian history prior to the sixteenth century. While the Great Schism is arguably the most tragic event in the history of Christianity and is addressed in any decent encyclopedia or book on medieval history, I had never read anything about it!

But here's what I discovered. Up until the eleventh century, the Church of Jesus Christ—even with growing tensions between East and West—was one, united Body. Just as Jesus promised she would, she stood against fierce and powerful heretical challenges and had persevered across ten centuries, keeping intact the Apostolic Faith. But in 1054, the Church was torn in two from within. This Great Schism resulted over basically two large issues, and other smaller ones. First, the bishop of Rome had decided, on his own, apart from his colleagues in the East, that he should have preeminence above all other bishops. He unilaterally decreed, without the approval of an ecumenical council, that by right of his ordinational descent from Peter, he should have authority over all other bishops—and be the "bishops' bishop," if you will.

Secondly, the Church in the West decided to change the Nicene Creed. The First and Second Ecumenical Councils (in 325 and 381) had established that creed as the definitive statement of Christian belief. The Creed of Nicea states that Christ is the Only-Begotten Son of God the Father, and that the Holy Spirit proceeds from the Father. In the West, the Creed had been altered to include the phrase known historically as the *filioque* clause. This changed our understanding of the Person of the Holy Spirit, saying that He proceeds from the Father *and the Son.*

Bishops from the Eastern regions protested this as a demotion of the Spirit from His place of co-equality with the Father and the Son. After all, Jesus taught that the Holy Spirit proceeds from the Father (John 15:26). They also challenged the bishop of Rome's claim to primacy. The ancient tradition of the Church would have demanded a council be called. But this did not happen.

Instead, the *filioque* was adopted in the West, and the pope of Rome set himself up as God's supreme authority on earth. In 1054, he excommunicated the patriarch of Constantinople, who refused to follow him. Who did and who didn't join with the pope fell pretty much along the dividing line between Western and Eastern Europe. And there, in the middle of the eleventh century, emerged not the Catholic Church, but the *Roman* Catholic Church. The Eastern Church became known as the Orthodox Church (from *ortho*, meaning "right" or "true," and *doxa*, meaning "glory").

I'd heard of the Orthodox Church, of course. But in my mind, I guess I'd always assumed Orthodox people were just Greek and Russian Catholics. Now I was discovering that while Roman Catholicism and Orthodoxy have the same root—that glorious first-millennium Church—the Orthodox Church claims to be the living, unchanged continuation of that Ancient Faith. It declares itself to be that Body in which the promise of Christ to forever preserve His Church remains fulfilled.

Without delay, I began to read about Orthodoxy. I learned that while the Roman Church has become home to many questionable beliefs and practices (like purgatory and indulgences), the Eastern Church has remained steadfast to those ancient teachings of the Faith I had embraced as the truth. It even maintains the same conciliar method of Church government that I saw revealed in the Scriptures and the Councils.

Again, I was flabbergasted by my own ignorance. I felt even worse when I mentioned my new interest in Orthodoxy to a philosopher colleague of mine. When I told him what I'd been studying, he said, "Ah, yes. Eastern Orthodoxy. You know, one must remember that it was against *Roman* aberrations that the Protestant Reformers rebelled. It seems eminently clear to me that if Martin Luther had sought out the Eastern Orthodox, there never would have been a Protestant Reformation. He would have had nothing to complain about." This man is by his own admission not even a Christian! How could I have been so unenlightened about Orthodoxy?

But unfortunately, in leaving Roman Catholicism, Luther did not reunite with the Ancient Faith (although some of his followers flirted with the idea [3]). Instead, he and the other Reformers created a new faith, founded upon newly engineered aberrations like *sola scriptura*. The terrible inadequacies of that doctrine I had come to understand extremely well.

Orthodoxy, and Home

It wasn't much later that I attended an Orthodox church for the first time in my life. At the beginning of the Liturgy, the priest faced the altar. In a strong and victorious voice, he sang, "Blessed is the Kingdom of the Father, and of the Son, and of the Holy Spirit, now and ever, and unto the ages of ages." The choir and congregation responsively sang a glorious "Amen."

As those joyous words poured forth, I was suddenly engulfed in that loving Presence for which I had spent a lifetime searching. Jesus Christ was filling my heart; and all around me, flowing like the divine oil of gladness from every word and act, was the truth of the Ancient Faith, unchanged in two thousand years. By the mercy of Christ, I'd always somehow known that when I found the real *truth*, I would find real *love*. After all, *Truth* is not a *thing;* it is a *Person*. And that *Person*, the Incarnate Son of God, is infinite *Love*.

Standing there in that blessed moment, Truth and Love washing over my soul, I was reminded of the question Jesus had posed to me nearly thirty years before, at the beginning of this long and arduous journey: *Matthew, is what you believe the truth?* At last—at long, long last—I felt I had an answer for Him. Surrounded by the incense and the beautiful prayers of the Liturgy, I looked through my tears toward the altar and whispered, *Yes, Lord, it is.*

And as clearly as I have ever heard words spoken, He answered silently, *Matthew, you are home.*

Part II

Rite and Wrong

→ 7 ←

Love Beyond Reason

At that Liturgy, my life with Christ truly began. Now, how can someone who has been a serious Christian for nearly forty years possibly say something like that? It's because Orthodox Christianity placed in my hands that mysterious "something" I'd been searching for all my life. From the ancient Faith, you see, I was at last learning how to really love God.

In the Book of Ephesians, St. Paul considers the great mystery of our relationship with God. In the fifth chapter, the Apostle teaches that the deep mystery of our union with God is best portrayed by the mystery of marriage, in which a man and woman become "one flesh" (Ephesians 5:31, 32).

I am eternally grateful to God that He has blessed me with the entirely undeserved and inexpressible joy of knowing what it is to be "one flesh" with my wonderful wife. After twenty-five years, I find it is nearly impossible to reflect for more than a moment or two upon my beloved Alice without getting a little misty. Sometimes I feel so close to her, I cannot tell where my soul ends, and hers begins. I don't even have to see her walk into a room to know that she's there. There are intimate times when the beautiful feelings between us defy all earthly description; for in those moments, the power and purity of our love touches a world beyond this one.

So this is what comes to mind when I think of real love. But in the great Mystery of Love, my bond with Alice is a pale and impoverished shadow when compared to the oneness that I can share with Christ. He illumines my soul and drives me to my unworthy knees in repentant gratitude and joy. The very thought of Him can engender affectionate and thankful tears. More and more, as I live in the consuming beauty of His overwhelming love, I find my earthly desires, hopes, and commitments taking on the transitory substance of dreams.

When one knows this kind of love, it is not hard to comprehend how a man can joyfully gather up his chains and march unfalteringly into the pit of torturers or into the jaws of beasts. We see such ineffable oneness with Christ in the lives of the Apostles and martyrs. As a Protestant, I'd had a taste of it in the first love of my conversion and at other pivotal moments on my spiritual journey.

The truth is, most sincere Protestants I know have had similar experiences. They recall them with unique fondness and joy. Unfortunately, what makes these times so special is the fact that they are so rare. They are not part of the everyday routine of evangelical life.

Yet the devoted Protestants I know long to revisit those moments, just as I did. They depend on their preachers and teachers to help them get back to "the good old days" of their first-love encounters with Christ. They look to stirring salvation messages, inspiring music, insightful books, and intimate retreats to help them reignite that special flame in their souls. Sometimes, they do experience a revival of that love. But as every sincere Protestant I know will attest, the rekindled flame eventually ebbs.

In becoming Orthodox, I learned two very important things about first love, about the kind of love that permeated the lives of the early Christians. First of all, I learned that one *can* live each day in that experience. I don't have to be constantly trying to get back to it. For a serious Orthodox believer, first love can become everyday love, and in the next chapter I will try to describe this process.

What's more, I learned that the path to a profound and eternally deepening love relationship with Jesus is actually a very simple, humble, and quiet one. It calls for dedication, yes. But it doesn't require exciting concerts, inspirational bestsellers, intensive Bible-study courses, or moving sermons.

So what does Orthodoxy have that Protestantism doesn't? Why can't Protestant faith consistently experience Christ in the way it so devoutly desires? In becoming Orthodox, I discovered the problem with my Protestant faith lay in the fact that the way it taught me to relate to God just didn't work.

You see, the Protestant way of living in Christ is thoroughly rooted in a system of thinking known as *rationalism.* In this chapter, I will seek to show how this rationalism prevents even the most dedicated Protestant believer from truly living in his first love.

Rationalism

When I talk about *rationalism,* or about being *rationalistic,* I am *not* referring simply to the process of thinking in a rational, lucid, intelligent, sensible way. There is nothing "irrational" about Orthodoxy. In fact, when a person opens his heart to it, he finds that nothing in the world is more reasonable or more sensible than the ancient Faith.

When we speak of *rationalism,* we are instead talking about *a particular way of seeing things.* Rationalism is an historical worldview that has influenced Western thinking, including Protestant thinking, since the time of Plato. Its essential tenet is that truth is discovered through *reasoning,* not through *experience* (that is, through observations, feelings, or actions).

For instance, in one of the first sermons I can remember, the preacher held his Bible high over his head, waved it for emphasis, and cried, "When it comes to your faith in God, you can't trust in your *eyes.* You can't trust in your *ears.* You can't trust in your *feelings.* All you can trust in is what you *know* from the Word of God!"

I also remember lots of exciting conversations with Protestant friends in which we eagerly shared with one another the things that the Lord had been showing us in the Bible. We measured the intimacy of our experiences with Christ by the depth of our theological understanding. Clearly, growing in the Lord primarily meant perceiving new information about Him.

More recently, a friend of mine who is a Protestant pastor told me of a discussion he'd had with some other Protestant ministers. It seems that they were all considering taking some classes in logic and critical thinking. When I asked what had led them to this decision, he told me that they had all reached the conclusion that, when a person is struggling spiritually, the problem is really in that person's *thinking.* So they thought some education in thinking logically would be of benefit in their pastoral duties.

Rational understanding is the ground of faith for every sincere Protestant. His spiritual experience is built upon prayerful, methodical study of the Bible. He fervently plumbs the depths of its pages, using every commentary, encyclopedia, reference book, and study aid at his disposal. As one Bible teacher used to say, he tries to get his "Bible doctrine in the frontal lobe." The hope is that with each new nugget of biblical wisdom unearthed, the believer's understanding of Christ will grow, and in turn his love for Him will deepen.

Now, it was a bit of a shock for me to learn through my studies that this approach to faith was foreign to the early Church. It makes sense, though. For openers, almost no one then had access to the books that later became the New Testament. If the truth about God could only be discovered through reason and knowledge, these early believers would have been left out.

But instead, the Church held to a *sacramental* view of Christian life. Sacramentalism is the belief that truth is discovered by *experiencing* the living Presence of Christ, by participating with Him in specific acts of worship that He Himself ordains.

The Reformers, and especially their followers, generally rejected this way of the early Church. [1] Instead, they looked at the Bible through rational eyes and said, "We will come to know the truth about God only through our study of the Holy Scriptures. Our experiences are untrustworthy and irrational teachers. Only through our knowledge of the Word of God can He reveal Himself to us and enter into our lives." They saw this as the only way to correct the errors of Rome, who they believed had substituted her own traditions for the Scriptures.

Of course, the Reformers would say that feelings and actions are still important. As Christians, our feelings must be pure, our actions righteous. But they would insist that right actions and right feelings *start* with the right understanding that produces them.

Head Knowledge, Heart Knowledge

There is one particular dilemma with which I think all Protestants are familiar and which demonstrates this understanding of things. How many sermons do you suppose have been preached on the old "head knowledge, heart knowledge" problem? After all, no question is of greater import in the life of the serious Protestant believer than: "How do I get the theological knowledge in my head to become love for God in my heart?"

How does this problem demonstrate rationalism in Protestant faith? Well, a Protestant takes it for granted that knowledge somehow becomes love. What's in the heart must first be in the head. That's rationalism, pure and simple.

Protestant believers also know this: The reason there are so many sermons preached about the "head knowledge, heart knowledge" problem is that moving things that short distance from the head to the heart seems to be an intrinsically difficult thing to do. We try all kinds of things. We bathe our souls with inspiring Christian music. We listen attentively at the feet of the most captivating Bible teachers. In our prayers and meditations, we conjure up images of Christ dying on the Cross. We envision ourselves as the lost lamb in His arms. We mentally try to look into His eyes as he struggles up the hill toward Golgotha. And sometimes, we are moved to feel something deep in our souls. But sooner or later—after a minute, an hour, a day, a week—it is gone again.

Why is this? When I discovered Orthodoxy, I found the answer. It had been right there in front of my eyes, all the years I lived the Protestant life. You see, anyone who will stop for a moment and simply consider *what love is* will realize that turning knowledge into love is an impossible endeavor. Head knowledge cannot become heart knowledge! Knowledge cannot produce love. It may direct us toward love. But it is not the same as love, nor can it serve as a substitute.

St. Paul is so clear about this fact that I don't know why I didn't see it long ago. I've discovered, though, that my modern mindset often kept me from seeing the obvious. St. Paul tells his spiritual children that the love we experience with Christ "passes knowledge" (Ephesians 3:19). The word "passes" is the Greek word that means "to transcend, surpass, or excel."

If we honestly reflect on our own life experiences, I think most of us will attest that love is a meeting of souls that far exceeds the scope of knowledge. Love is first and foremost the experience of another's life. Experiencing someone is entirely different from knowing about him. What the ancient Faith understands is that this is just as true with God as with His children.

The Doorway to Love

Since the point I'm trying to make is one about love, let me illustrate it with an analogy from my marriage. Imagine that I live in a room right next door to Alice. We've never met, however. That's a little odd, given the fact that there's a door between the two rooms where we reside. It's just that I've not been able to open it.

One day, someone tells me about this beautiful creature who lives on the other side of the wall. In a general way, he describes many of her qualities to me. For instance, I'm told that she is of medium height and slender build, works as a medical professional, and is a fine musician.

Now, I'm mysteriously intrigued by the thought of this woman behind the door. I think about her constantly. Frequently I stand in front of the door and try to envision her, given what I know. Often, I will talk to her through the door.

Gradually, a vivid image forms in my mind. I see a lady who stands 5'6", weighs about 120 pounds, is a nurse, and plays acoustic guitar. I am entirely smitten with my image of this woman. I want to enter into a loving relationship with her.

Now, let's consider this. Suppose that in actuality, the Alice "beyond the door" is not a 5'6", 120-pound, guitar-playing nurse. She's actually a 5'4", 100-pound ophthalmic technician. When it comes to guitars, she's clueless. But she does play a mean accordion!

If that's the case, how useful would we say that all my study and meditation on Alice's description has been in bringing me into a genuine love relationship with her? Obviously, it has not contributed much. In fact, all those mistaken notions could actually get in the way of my establishing a relationship with the real Alice, if and when I finally do meet her. They could keep me from recognizing who she really is.

Next, let's suppose that in my careful study and rational analysis of her dossier, I've actually come to a nearly perfect picture of the Alice next door. Even though I've never seen her, I'm captivated by her. I'm even correct in my assumption that she is taken with me (for, just as I suspect, she has *my* description as well).

Now, I certainly may seem to be in a better spot concerning Alice than I was when I pictured her incorrectly. But let me ask this question: Does my completely correct *understanding* of Alice and her thoughts about me amount to a genuine *love relationship* with Alice?

Even here, the answer is clearly "No." The simple fact is that I can't have a real loving relationship with a mental image of someone I have not actually experienced—no matter how accurate that image may be. True love requires a live encounter with another person. It demands an interaction with that person that encompasses heart, soul, mind, and body.

I could spend every moment of my life in front of the door between Alice and me. I could scrutinize the finest details of her description. I could conjure up the most vivid images of her. In the end, it would actually make no difference whether the conclusions I reached about her were accurate or mistaken. In either case, my rationalistic approach to knowing Alice could never establish me in a real loving relationship with her.

What must I do to truly love Alice? I think it's fairly obvious. I must open the door and embrace her! All my studying and imagining could never be a substitute for holding her, being with her. In experiencing her, I will come to know with certainty who she is—in a way I never could through my rational meditations.

Of course, this analogy is meant to show the problems with the rationalistic Protestant approach to God. So instead of Alice, let's make it Jesus on the other side of the door. Instead of a dossier to study, I have the Scriptures. Nevertheless, everything that was true with Alice is true with Him. A lifetime of study and meditation about Christ will never accomplish what needs to be done if I am really to experience Him. I must open the door and embrace Christ as a Person, not as an object of my theological imagination.

The flaw at the heart of Protestant faith is this: Protestant faith does not really know *how*—in any consistent way—to get free of its rationalizing, open the door, and experience Jesus. That's what leaves devoted Protestants constantly seeking revival. It's what keeps them going to the Christian bookstore, looking for titles that promise to unlock the secret to a deep relationship with God. They yearn for a day-to-day experience of the richness of Christ's living Presence. But their faith can't give them that.

The Idea of God

Now, at this point, I can hear my Protestant friends saying, "But wait! What happened when I gave my heart to Christ? I heard Him at the door, knocking (Revelation 3:20). And I asked Him into my life. Are you telling me I didn't really open the door to Him? Are you saying I didn't experience Him in a real, living way when that happened?"

No, I'm not saying that at all. The truth is, I would not be Orthodox today were it not for the fact that Jesus graciously revealed Himself to me while I was a Protestant. I believe that the Lord always finds a way to communicate an awareness of His Person to honest, truth-seeking souls, whoever and wherever they are.

But I'd like my Protestant readers to reflect with me about those special moments with Christ—at the altar when we gave Him our hearts, and in those other tearful, joyous, and peace-filled moments when we've had a profound sense that He is *real*. Let me ask: Is that realness something a person *thinks*, or *feels*?

I think we'd all say our richest experiences with God are felt in our hearts, not thought in our minds. What's more, they seem to happen outside of and apart from our rationalistic routine of getting our "Bible doctrine in the frontal lobe." For instance, at the hour of their conversion, many people know very little about God; and yet many would say that's the moment in which Christ's presence is most deeply felt.

Yes, at such times the voice of Christ calling from beyond the door, and His warmth emanating through the door, compel us to open the door—the door of the heart—to Him. We stand there beholding Him.

So why do those precious moments with Him always fade? Why don't they last? It's because Protestant rationalism teaches us that the way to really encounter Christ is to study about Him. So sooner or later, the Protestant believer must turn His attention from the Jesus who is simply *there* to the Jesus of his scriptural interpretations. In terms of my analogy, he turns away from the Christ standing in the doorway, to the Christ in a dossier. He lets the door close on the *Person* of Christ, to focus on his *idea* of Christ.

That idea, while perhaps compelling and motivating, is no substitute for the Person. What's more, it bears the mark of the believer's own interpretations. As we saw in my analogy, that may thwart his relationship with the real Christ as much as it may help it. It may actually prevent the believer from truly recognizing Him.

Interestingly, C. S. Lewis clearly saw the implications of trading the Person of Christ for one's own idea of Christ. In *The Screwtape Letters*, the Archfiend Screwtape advises his nephew demon Wormwood to look into the mind of the Christian man he is trying to deceive. When that man prays, to what does he typically direct his prayers? Is it to a divine Person? No, Screwtape says. When you look in his mind,

> you will not find *that*. If you examine the object to which he is attending, you will find that it is a composite object containing many quite ridiculous ingredients. . . . But whatever the nature of the composite object, you must keep him praying to *it*—to the thing that he has made, not to the Person who has made him.[2]

Finding the Love

Looking back, I realize that my Protestant rationalism forced me to live in a restless tension between an awareness of the beautiful reality of Christ and a faith that does not know how to experience Him as He is. Of course, I'm not the only Protestant who's ever come face-to-face with the shortcomings of his rationalistic faith.

At a ministerial conference I attended years ago, the most touching speaker of the entire week was an elderly seminary professor who had given sixty years of his life to ministry. About half an hour into an inspiring sermon laden with a lifetime of theological insights, this frail old man abruptly stopped and bowed his head. Everyone was taken aback. After a few moments, he lifted his head, declaring soberly, "You know, folks, there are times when I wish I could forget everything I've ever learned about God and about the Scriptures, and just go back to that moment when I first met Jesus."

As that elderly professor had discovered, one who desires nothing more than to stand in the doorway and embrace the living Christ will ultimately find the Protestant path a disappointment. It can't be otherwise, since the keys to that kind of life are among the things that the Reformers discarded as they created their new vision of the Church.

So my greatest joy, when I encountered original Christianity, was to find that Orthodoxy still holds those keys. It knows full well how to embrace God as He is. The ancient Church understands how to love Jesus Christ as a living Person, not as a collection of great theological ideas.

What is it that allows Orthodox Christians to have a live encounter with God? It is the sacraments—those blessed rites of worship by which we touch the living Person of Christ. Anyone who walks the sacramental path that the true Church has walked from Pentecost to the present day may come to know Jesus Christ as a real and intimate "heavenly Lover."[3]

→ 8 ←

A Living Salvation

So what is the Orthodox sacramental path? What makes it such a different way to God?

One thing is for sure: Orthodoxy does not teach a person to experience God by putting his faith in some modern idea of God that he's chosen to believe. The Orthodox believer knows that reason and understanding are not the keys to a spiritual encounter with the living Person of Christ. He would never try to defend or explain his relationship with Christ by appealing to his own subjective convictions about his personal interpretations of the Scriptures.

Instead, the Orthodox Christian devotes himself to certain acts of love designed to open the heart's door and allow him to encounter Jesus Christ as He is. These acts were taught to the early Church by the Apostles and have been practiced by Christ's true Body since Pentecost. By performing them, the believer stands in the doorway, experiencing the Presence of Christ with his heart, his mind, and his body.

Rather than look to rational proofs and theological arguments, the Orthodox believer finds the confirmation of his faith in the proven, verifiable spiritual history of these blessed traditions, called *sacraments*. Performing these acts within the holy community of the Church gives the believer the opportunity to encounter the living Presence of Christ.

This is a way of life totally removed from the Protestant path of studying and refining beliefs. One who travels the sacramental path does not focus upon learning more *about* God, in hope that this knowledge will somehow miraculously turn into true love. Rather, day by day, moment by moment, the believer participates directly in Christ's life by joining Him in the sacramental acts of love that He Himself has ordained we perform together.

This way to God is founded upon a simple, fundamental truth: real love is an *act,* not an idea. When I meet God by participating with Him in an uncomplicated act, I can experience Him purely, fully, without my self-created ideas and images getting in the way. When I'm doing something with God, there is no room for interpreting Him, or forcing Him into the mold of my idea of Him.

Let me illustrate my point this way. There's a sense in which participating in a sacrament is like taking Jesus' hand and stepping off a precipice. Out there in midair, my imagination, my interpretations, and my preconceived notions about Christ have no effect on anything. All I can do is focus my total attention on Him, wait upon Him, and experience whatever He does. In this respect, sacraments are pure acts of faith; and in the midst of that faith, Christ shows Himself.

In this chapter, I want to introduce my reader to the sacramental path of the ancient Christian Faith. With all my heart, I pray that those who long to love Christ will see the reality of this way. For when one in faith embraces it, he opens himself to unfathomable encounters with Divine Love.

Understanding Sacraments

Most Christians, of course, are familiar with the word *sacrament.* Many even know that the ancient Church generally identifies seven major sacraments: Baptism, Chrismation (anointing for receiving the Holy Spirit), the Holy Eucharist (Communion), Confession (otherwise called the Sacrament of Repentance), Ordination, Marriage (yes, marriage is a sacrament!), and Holy Unction (anointing with oil for healing).

These are the seven major sacraments, so to speak. They are acts, biblical acts, in which we experience God and His grace. But there are many other practices of the Faith that could be considered sacramental. In fact, an Orthodox believer would say that the whole Christian life is sacramental. Prayer, fasting, the reading of the Scriptures, and the veneration of saints are among the many other Spirit-inspired acts that Orthodox Christianity has preserved since the days of the Apostles. They shape literally every aspect of an

Orthodox believer's life; his work, his play, his eating, his sleeping, his relationships, even his sense of time—all are ordered by sacramental acts of communion with God.

Again, from the greatest to the smallest, the thing that all of these worship practices have in common is that they are *actions*. They are not ideas, or beliefs, or doctrines, or concepts. They are the keys to an *experiential* relationship with Christ in His Holy Church.

Let me underscore two important points. First, sacraments play a crucial role in salvation. For as the ancient Church understands, salvation is not a matter of merely trusting in certain beliefs. Rather, it is a process of transformation that occurs as one sacramentally encounters the living Presence of Christ. Secondly, this process of salvation must be anchored in the Church through acts or (bear with me) rituals revealed to us by Christ Himself.

Unfortunately, even the Protestant who wants to understand these things faces a formidable obstacle. You see, there are ways in which the sacramental path and the path of Protestant rationalism move in opposite directions. For instance, for a Protestant, spiritual experience is a result of spiritual understanding. Conversely, for an Orthodox Christian, spiritual understanding is a result of spiritual experience.

We see an example of this difference in the practice of Communion. Most Protestants take Communion as a way of demonstrating outwardly that they hold to a belief in the saving grace of Christ and in His return. But for the Orthodox Christian, taking Communion is a holy moment in which he encounters the living Christ through the God-embracing Sacrament. Contemplating that experience leads him into a deeper understanding of Christ.

So for the Protestant, the purpose of the Communion experience is to demonstrate that he already understands something; but for the Orthodox Christian, understanding comes as a result of the Communion experience. This "reverse emphasis" often makes it hard for a Protestant to comprehend the sacramental way. Understanding it may prove to be a bit like trying to drive a car across town in reverse, looking only in the rear-view mirror.

The necessity of ritual in our lives with God is also a difficult point for a Protestant to grasp. Due to his rationalism, he can't help but see Christian faith in terms of *concepts* and *ideas*. So the minute you begin to talk about acts and experiences—like formal, liturgical worship, or praying from a prayer book, or venerating icons, or lighting candles, or fasting, or any other sacramental practice—the Protestant sighs and declares, "That stuff is all just empty ritual! It's 'works religion'!"

I shared that view. It's a completely understandable reaction. For the Protestant, growing in love for God requires gaining new information about Him. That's why Protestants flock to churches with preachers who are great at presenting fresh, biblical, motivational thoughts about God (or at least, do a good job of presenting old ideas in uplifting ways). Obviously, to one whose life with God is built primarily on encountering new and stimulating things to think about, the sacramental life—doing the same old ritualistic things, over and over again—will appear entirely empty.

Somehow, the Protestant who wants to understand the sacramental path of the ancient Church must fathom that these rituals are *anything* but empty. Instead, performing them allows one to have a live encounter with God. Do you know what happens every time an Orthodox Christian opens the door of his heart by practicing a sacrament, in faith and with a pure heart? He enters heaven! He embraces the living Christ! Now, tell me: if that's the same old experience that happens every time the believer does the same old ritualistic thing, why would he ever want to do anything different?

Still, all this is completely foreign to the typical Protestant. If he is ever to get a sense of the beauty of the sacramental life, he must see that the way of the early Church, the way of Orthodoxy, is an entirely different way of being with God from the one he has always endorsed. Most importantly, he must understand that as long as he tries to judge that sacramental path through the eyes of his deeply ingrained rationalism, he will never be able to see the divine love and wisdom that pervade it. The truth is, sacraments are about God's love for us. To comprehend them, a Protestant will have to study them, but with the eyes of his heart.

Let me return to the two points of difficulty I identified above. How does it alter one's view of faith and salvation when one recognizes that their foundation is a living, interactive, sacramental process, rather than a set of theological beliefs? My whole world changed when I finally saw that Christianity is a sacramental experience, not a philosophy. I will examine this issue first.

Then in the next chapter, I will turn to the whole question of ritual. My attempt there will be to point out something that the reader will probably find obvious, once he reflects awhile upon his own experiences of love. When he does so, he will see his own life proves that without ritual, love cannot exist.

A Living Salvation

One response I get quite often when I discuss the sacramental life with my Protestant friends is, "Why are you so concerned with *experiencing* God? After all, a person's salvation is not really based on the intensity of his relationship with God. Salvation was accomplished by Jesus on the Cross. His sacrifice justifies us. When you accept Him as your Savior, His righteousness is imputed to you. At that point, you're saved. It's the work of Christ on Calvary that will always be your salvation.

"None of that has anything to do with your experience of God. If you happen to have a really tender, loving relationship with God, well, that's wonderful. It's like the icing on the cake. But when it comes to salvation, experiencing God is not as critical a thing as you're making it out to be."

How well I know this version of the gospel. I lived it and preached it for forty years. But I came to see that my belief system had left me with an incorrect picture of what the Incarnation, life, death, and Resurrection of Jesus were all about. I discovered that just like everything else involving God, salvation is a dynamic, living, ongoing process.

Now, just like other Protestants, I used to see Christ's Incarnation as the means for God to accomplish certain goals. These objectives are fundamentally legal in nature. The plan of salvation, I'd been taught, is driven by God's need to maintain His holiness and justice, while providing merciful redemption for sinful man. Thus, Christ becomes man to teach us the good news of God's love, and to suffer for man the punishment that God's justice legally (in a divine sense) demands. By virtue of His death and Resurrection, a human being can, by faith, have his personal debt to God cancelled. This transaction allows God to graciously and justly accept that individual into His Kingdom.

To my great surprise, I discovered that the Apostles and the early Church did *not* understand the plan of salvation in this way. Oh, they certainly believed that human beings are guilty of betraying their Creator, and are deserving of eternal damnation. Of course, they believed that Jesus, in His sacrifice, brings pardon for us and mediates God's merciful reconciliation.

But the early Christians did not see salvation as a legal transaction, full of complex questions about justification and sanctification. They perceived salvation in a simpler, more tangible, more vibrantly loving way. For them, to be saved is not to have a new legal status before God. For them, the truly joyous good news of the Gospel is that by joining His nature to mine in the Incarnation, Christ can now join my nature to His. Thus, my blessed Lord and I may literally become *One* in His Body, the Church.

To be saved, then, is to be drawn into union with God, into the life of the Divine. It is to transcend the vileness, emptiness, and living death of our sin-infected lives by becoming wondrously united with Jesus Christ. Right now, we can begin to experience a life so interwoven with Christ's that eventually it will become difficult to distinguish between our two lives.

This was the glorious day-to-day experience that so empowered the first Christians. This is the relationship with God that St. Paul is describing when he writes that the life in each of us is not his own, but rather Christ's (Galatians 2:20). It is what he has in mind when he declares that our lives are "hidden" within the Christ who is Himself "our life" (Colossians 3:3, 4). Such is the life that devoted Orthodox believers live today.

Salvation cannot be merely some prize that I attained through making a commitment to Christ at church camp twenty years ago.

It is not a contract to which I can point and declare, "Hey, I've got my salvation!" Rather, it is the ongoing and living *process* of losing myself in the life of Christ in His Church. Unless I am willing to commit myself to that kind of vital experience with Him, I cannot effectively be His follower.

Jesus Himself vividly portrays this living salvation in His own parable of the vine and branches (John 15:1–6). He tells us that unless we are constantly abiding in Him in an intimate union, we will wither, die, and be lost from Him. From our Lord's own teaching we learn that having an experiential connection with Him is not just the "icing" on a salvation that is first and foremost a legal declaration from God. The fact is, a living relationship with Him *is* our salvation.

So the understanding of the Apostles and the ancient Church is that receiving Christ means inviting Him to come to us, nourish us, and graciously save us by His continuous mercy and love. Redemption is Christ joining Himself to us, changing and sanctifying our flesh, heart, mind, and soul. Salvation is *transformation.*

How Do We Love God?
Think of it: we are saved by *loving* God. As St. James reminds us, salvation in the Kingdom of Christ belongs only to "those who *love* Him" (James 1:12; 2:5, italics mine).

Thinking back on my Protestant life, I can remember many conversations and small gatherings where someone mustered the courage to ask, "*How* do we love God?" The Scriptures gave us a lot of information about God and about what our lives in Christ should be like. But they seemed very silent when it came to telling us exactly how to attain that life.

As a Protestant minister, I always felt a twinge of embarrassment for not being able to answer that question in a way that was really meaningful for anyone—including myself. Typically, when my Protestant friends and I would fumble with that question, some wistful person would eventually repeat a common old lament: "Don't you wish God would just send a letter down from heaven telling us exactly what we need to *do?*"

For anyone who's ever said that, I have great news. God has done precisely that! In the sacraments of His Holy Church, which have been practiced from apostolic times, God *has* clearly spelled out for us what we need to *do* to love Him. By performing these sacraments, one can escape the dead-end of rational religion and enter into a living communion with Christ.

Sacraments, then, are the Holy Spirit's "Do this!" to those people who long to love God deeply. What's more, these acts of love are not difficult to perform. So, in a wonderfully gentle, quiet, and natural way, anyone who, out of love for Christ, devotes himself to practicing the sacraments of the Orthodox Faith will find himself within the intimate, saving, transforming embrace of Jesus Christ our God.

→ 9 ←

The Right Ritual

Rituals—lighting candles, bowing down, making the sign of the Cross—are well-defined acts practiced over and over again, century after century, by God's people. Earlier, I pointed out that it is the ritual nature of sacraments that causes some people I know to write them off as "works religion." But in the next few pages, I intend to show that any act of worship that unites me intimately to Christ *must* be a ritual. Why? It's because love cannot exist *without* ritual.

Let me illustrate that. Alice makes the most incredible meatloaf in the Western Hemisphere. I mean this seriously: if given a choice between filet mignon and her meatloaf, I'll take the meatloaf every time.

The first time she served it to me twenty-five years ago, I told her, "Honey, this is the best meatloaf I've ever tasted!" It really was! I went on and on about how great it was. In fact, I think I embarrassed her with my excessive praise.

So, the next time she served meatloaf, she knew I was being playfully tongue-in-cheek when I contentedly sighed, "Oh, Alice, I don't know if I've ever told you this before, but you make the most fantastic meatloaf!" She laughed, and gave me a little kiss. I knew she was genuinely pleased at my appreciation.

A few nights ago, we had meatloaf. When she served it up, I gave her a wink. She shook her head, and chuckled. Then, just as I have done *every single time* that delicious morsel has appeared on our table in the last quarter-century, I said, "Alice, I don't know if I've ever told you this before, but. . ."

How can a plate of simple (but perfectly exquisite!) meatloaf become a point of intimate connection between two people? When it becomes the center of a ritual of love. Anyone who's lived in love with someone for half a lifetime can tell you that it's not the changes or the exciting surprises that create undying mutual devotion. These are nice, but not nearly as important as predictable day-to-day acts of love. That "I love you" at night, the kiss each morning, the shirts that are always laundered just right, the garbage that's taken out, the heartfelt poem written in each year's Valentine, the weekly break-fasts at our special place—these form the fiber and essence of our relationship. Without such repeated, predictable interactions, there is no ongoing love *story*.

Why? Because what makes love real is its constancy and its pre-dictability, not its occasional spikes and flutters. It is a powerful *sameness*, an invariability lying beneath all the changes and alter-ations of life. The experiences that allow us to touch, feed, and nur-ture that beautiful changelessness are the *ritual acts of love* that we perform with the ones we love.

The Rituals of God

This is especially true in a relationship with God. Here, one partner is the incomprehensible Creator. The other is a blind and ignorant mortal. If God constantly moved the doors or changed the dance, we would never be able to keep up with Him. Most importantly, God by nature never changes. In His essential Being, He is unal-tered Sameness. "Jesus Christ is the same yesterday, today, and for-ever" (Hebrews 13:8).

This is important to recognize, for the simple reason that *wor-ship must reflect its object*. For instance, the worship of a God who is Love can only include acts of love. Just so, worship whose object is the unchangeable God must in itself be changeless in nature. Trying to touch Sameness through random acts of spontaneity (themselves designed to please the worshiper) is like my attempting to hold in an unbroken embrace someone who is standing immovably on solid ground, while I myself am standing on a revolving carousel.

So everywhere throughout history, the eternal unchanging God is worshiped in ritual that He establishes. This was true in the Old Testament and the New. And it is certainly true in heaven. In the fourth chapter of Revelation, we read:

The four living creatures, each having six wings, were full of eyes around and within. And *they do not rest day or night,* saying:
"Holy, holy, holy,
Lord God Almighty,
Who was and is and is to come!"

Whenever the living creatures give glory and honor and thanks to Him who sits on the throne . . . the twenty-four elders fall down before Him . . . and cast their crowns before the throne, saying:
"You are worthy, O Lord,
To receive glory and honor and power"
(Revelation 4:8–11, italics mine).

And what about here on earth? God gave to His people Israel a completely sacramental and ritualistic way of worship. Having been formed in that tradition, the Apostles knew no other way to relate to God. Neither did the Lord Jesus ever instruct those simple fishermen to create a new way of worship. He simply placed Himself at the center of their rituals. This is corroborated by the Book of Acts, in which we see the first Christians worshiping liturgically in the synagogue and observing the sacrament of the Eucharist[1] in their homes.

Later, writing in the middle of the second century, St. Justin Martyr reveals a Church whose sacramental ways, in all essential respects, are preserved today within the Holy Orthodox Church.[2] Today, the rituals of love bequeathed to the Church by the Holy Spirit through the Apostles—the sacraments—are still alive and well. They continue to unite believers in oneness with their heavenly Lover.

The charge that ritual worship is somehow an attempt to work one's way into heaven is utterly unfounded. The Orthodox Church knows better than anyone that we are saved by the *mercy* of God, not by our *works*. Virtually every one of our prayers contains the plea, "Lord have mercy."

No, by our sacramental rituals we open ourselves to the transforming power of oneness that Christ brings to those whom He saves. Through them, Jesus accomplishes the purpose for which He has saved us. Since His purposes have always been the same, it is easy to see why the rituals of love that Christ has instilled in His Church would never change. What we also need to see, however, are the dangers inherent in changing those sacramental traditions.

"New" Rituals

Let me go back for a moment to marriage, as a God-given ritual. All serious believers would say that God's intent for marriage is the joining together of a man and woman in Christ, for a lifetime. The biblical standard requires that man and that woman to remain celibate until marriage; the norm thereafter demands their faithfulness to one another. The ritual act of sexual intercourse between husband and wife serves both as the God-ordained expression of their love for each other, and as the means for the blessing of children. We might call this the traditional way of approaching and experiencing Christian marriage.

But today this marriage scenario is confused by endless changes and innovations. Think of the major alterations that have occurred just in my lifetime. In the 1960s, two things changed. First divorce got easier, with the institution of no-fault laws. Next, unmarried sex permeated society under the labels of "free love" and "meaningful relationships."

Consider also the progression in modern terminology for what Scripture simply calls "fornication." We went from "making love" to "having sex," and now we just call it "hooking up." Each phrase moves farther away from the rhetoric of the norm. When you change the rules, you change the words. But we're not through.

Once the sanctity of sex between men and women went by the boards, it was a short hop to an accompanying acceptance of same-sex ritual in society. Pick up the daily want ads most anywhere in America and note the "men seeking men" and "women seeking women" sections. A Lutheran church in St. Paul, Minnesota, just ordained a lesbian pastor (against the rules of the denomination).

The Boy Scouts are criticized as exclusionary and discriminatory because they want to maintain their tradition of a heterosexual worldview, a right the Supreme Court has affirmed.

Looking at these altered sexual rituals in society, men and women who lived out the rituals of traditional sexuality say, "What's going on here?! This can't be right." To which those living together will respond, "But we're in love—this is right for us." The gay couple will talk of their "committed" relationship.

Shifting back to the rituals of worship, we unfortunately see some similar progressions. The Scriptures reveal the ancient traditions of the Church. People are brought to Christ in Holy Baptism and receive the Holy Spirit through the prayer and anointing with oil called Chrismation (Acts 8:14–17). Forgiveness of sin is realized in the Sacrament of Repentance, or Confession (James 5:16). One is sustained and nourished in Christ by partaking of His Body and Blood each Sunday in the solemn Sacrament of Communion (Acts 20:7). For over fifteen hundred years, apart from an isolated heretical sect here and there, these traditions were held intact. If you were a true believer in Christ, these were the things you *did*. Period!

Now, think about the alterations that have occurred in *these* rituals, many of them in my lifetime. To come to Christ, you merely walk down an aisle or pray a prayer or mail in a letter (preferably with a gift enclosed). Baptism? It's not necessary; it's really up to you. To experience the Holy Spirit, you attend a banquet at the Holiday Inn, or sit in a chair and get prayed over, or send off for a new book (preferably with a gift enclosed). Confession is purely private—and increasingly rare. Weekly Communion has become monthly or quarterly at best, and is practiced with little sense of its New Testament necessity or solemnity.

The bottom line is this: although they probably don't recognize it, with respect to the rituals of traditional biblical Christianity, today's evangelicals and charismatics have become full-blown liberals!

Of course, contemporary Protestants will be quick to defend their new "rituals." They will do so by insisting that the old rituals just aren't necessary—"Jesus doesn't need baptism to save me." Or, they may point out that their contemporary ways of doing things produce rich, meaningful feelings: "When the TV preacher prayed, I put my hands on the screen and felt the Holy Spirit fall upon me," or "At our home fellowship, our hearts are warmed when we sit in a circle and pass around the Lord's Supper."

I cannot judge the meaningfulness of another's experience. But I can say that such practices are radical departures from the holy rituals of the New Testament and the historic Church. We modern Christians have changed the ways the unchanging God has deigned for us to approach Him.

Here's another thing I can say about Protestant worship rituals: whether they're conservative or liberal, whether they've been observed for five hundred years or were instituted by the pastor just last week, these practices clearly get in the way of Christ's desires for those whom He loves. They prevent the fulfillment of His prayer "that they all may be one, as You, Father, are in Me, and I in You" (John 17:21).

Let me illustrate this point. Suppose one day an edict is published proclaiming that anyone desiring to go to Christian Sunday services must attend the Pentecostal church—one where dancing in the aisles and speaking in tongues is the tradition. No other denomination will be permitted to hold services. What happens when Sunday morning rolls around? Will the Baptists and Lutherans turn out in droves? Very unlikely. Some will stay away because they feel they would find the worship distasteful. But others, perhaps most, will stay away because of a deeper conviction that the worship is wrong—or at least lacking in spirituality.

We could make the Pentecostals and the Baptists attend the Lutheran church. Or we could make the Pentecostals and Lutherans go to the Baptist church. We'd see the same problems. Similar attitudes of reluctance and inability to join heartily in the worship would hold in each case.

Here's the point. The varied, nontraditional rituals of contemporary Protestants divide Christians in their worship of God. If believers cannot without reservation unite their hearts in worship to God, can they ever be one with each other? If they cannot be one with each other, can they ever really be one with God?

In my Protestant days, we all wanted to be one with God. But a necessary requirement for that—being one with each other—was one we could never fulfill. Now, I can see the situation as analogous to two married people trying to become one flesh, but in constant disagreement about their acts of love and intimacy.

So we cooked up a phrase: unity in diversity. But you know what? There's no such thing. The word *di*-versity itself implies division—differing forms of worship *divide* the Body of Christ. This is not God's desire, and He must not be held responsible for it. Diversity in Christian worship can only be the product of self-directed, self-concerned individualism, and the multiplied thousands of denominations in Christendom are ample evidence to support that allegation.

Opening God's Doorways

Of course, the crucial thing about the sacraments of the ancient Orthodox Faith is that God has commanded them. By His Spirit, He has ordained *those particular acts* as the means for opening the doorway of the heart to Him. What's more, the simple fact that all His children must perform these very same acts naturally encourages oneness in His Church.

But let me be perfectly clear about two things. First, the sacraments are not made spiritually valid because everybody likes doing them. Remember where Jesus instructs, "Most assuredly, I say to you, unless you eat the flesh of the Son of Man and drink His blood, you have no life in you" (John 6:53). He continues, "Whoever eats My flesh and drinks My blood has eternal life, and I will raise him up at the last day" (v. 54).

Some of His followers responded, "This is a hard saying; who can understand it?" (v. 60). Today, some of His followers might say, "Surely He didn't *really* mean His body and blood." But the group in the Gospel story understood that He *did* mean it. That's why, as St. John observes, "From that time many of His disciples went back and walked with Him no more" (v. 66).

As Christians, we are not sacramental because that's the way we like to worship. We're sacramental because this is the path God has revealed and has commanded His Church to follow. In fact, let me be very candid for a moment. A Protestant who chooses to join himself to the ancient Church and its sacramental way will find himself encountering spiritual conflicts and struggles of a magnitude he's never faced before. To walk the sacramental path is to live every day in a Kingdom that is "not of this world" (John 18:36). From experience, I can tell you that a serious Orthodox Christian finds himself at odds with this sinful world, and with the sinful blackness of his own heart, to a depth and intensity unknown to most Protestant believers. Tears are his familiar companion. But through his sacramental life of struggle, he also comes to know unimaginable grace, overwhelming peace, inexpressible joy, indescribable love—and *true victory*. I will have more to say about this point in the last chapter.

Secondly, sacraments are not magic. These rituals of faith bring one who performs them into the Presence of God only because God has ordained it to be so. In order for communion with God to occur, the Church—and each believer—must perform these acts out of faithful obedience.

Christ did not give these blessed sacraments to individuals, to celebrate willy-nilly, wherever and however they pleased. These acts are done *within the community of the Church*. For the sacraments are not only meant to establish oneness between an individual believer and his Lord. They also form the fabric of a godly union between the members of the Body of Christ. It is through the sacraments that Christ makes His Church universal and One.

So why can't I just start my own independent group (like they did in Western Europe five hundred years ago), perform the sacraments, and thereby consider myself a valid part of the Christian tradition?

When an Orthodox Christian parish performs the sacraments of the Faith, it does so within the unbroken historical context of that very Church which received them at the start from the Holy Spirit. While some groups may mimic those rites almost perfectly, they do so as the descendants of people who willingly separated themselves from the ancient Church that the sacraments were meant to preserve as a single Body.

As I mentioned earlier, I see no problem with Martin Luther and the other Reformers protesting the errant practices of the sixteenth-century Roman Church. But in their course of action, they committed their own critical mistakes. Under the rationale of *sola scriptura,* they gave themselves the authority to pick and choose from the doctrines and practices of ancient Christianity.

Luther and the other Reformers did not think to ask that a council address their questions and doctrinal proposals, as was the practice of the Apostolic Church they claimed to represent. On no one's authority but their own, the Reformers declared themselves to be God's voices, even though they themselves could not agree as to what God was saying. In this, they ignored the Apostolic Church's principles of conciliar Church government and commitment to single-mindedness in doctrine. They turned from the ways of the Faith they were claiming to champion.

Even more basically, the Reformers were protesting the doctrines and practices of a Roman patriarch who some five hundred years earlier had himself separated from the other four patriarchs in Christendom, unilaterally going his own way. Thus, one writer has called that pope "the first Protestant"! Under the Reformation, Western Europe was exiting Rome in much the same fashion as Rome had exited the communion of the unbroken universal Church in the eleventh century.

The Reformers may have been sincere and well meaning. Especially in those churches that adopted a sacramental approach, an attempt was made to preserve a resemblance to the early Church. But what the Reformers really did was to recreate the Church of Christ according to their own vision of how things should be.

Thus, even those modern Protestants who embrace the sacraments do so as ones who have unfortunately found themselves planted outside that Apostolic Church to which the sacraments were given. How do I say this without offense? To stand outside the Church and practice its sacraments is analogous to a young man standing in a pasture, knocking baseballs over the fence and imagining himself in Yankee Stadium. He may be a committed athlete and have all that it takes to be a Yankee—the bat, the ball, the glove, even the required skill. But until he is actually on the team, he is playing fantasy baseball.

One may see himself as part of the true Church because he practices a sacramental way of life. Yet because he refrains from actually being joined to that true Church, he stands as an obstacle to the oneness Christ desires in His Body. Since a lack of oneness with the Body contributes to a lack of oneness with God, his faith remains a shadow of what it could be.

Where Is Oneness?

Because they have no connection to the God-ordained sacraments of the original Church, Protestant worship rituals cannot nurture oneness within the Body of Christ. I *think* most Protestants recognize that, which is why they tend to focus on the personal side of worship: those aspects of worship that are meant to connect the individual with God. But the same rites of worship that keep Protestants from being one with each other also keep individual believers from attaining true union with God.

→ 10 ←

"Just Jesus and Me"

So what is a Protestant to do? What steps can be taken when he sees that real oneness of worship with all other believers (Protestant or otherwise) is an impossibility? I mean, despite the spirit of Protestant ecumenism, and the growing number of denominational mergers going on these days, the prospects for Protestants ever being *one* are bleak. The fact that so many Protestants are *adamantly opposed* to Protestant ecumenism and church mergers confirms that!

My initial response was, "All I can do is worship God in a way that makes me feel near to Him. I can't be responsible for what the Body of Christ does. I can only be responsible for my own relationship with God."

Given the situation, that seems like an inescapable conclusion. But sadly, anyone can see that statement is full of self-concerned individualism. Such individualism thwarts God's desire for oneness in the Body. It also prevents true oneness between God and the individual. Thus, even the most sincere Protestant believer finds himself stuck in an irresolvable spiritual dilemma when it comes to his worship of God.

Why does he end up there? Let us consider. We all know that self-love is a source of sin. To free us from our preoccupation with self is one of God's chief purposes. I think of the oft-presented image, particularly popular in the seventies, of "taking myself off the throne of my life" and putting God there.

It wasn't until I began studying the Orthodox faith, however, that I realized how subtly and completely self-love permeates my life. Sometimes it cleverly disguises itself in forms that are not quite so stark and ugly as self-love. When I am self-concerned, when I practice self-justification, when I act on self-desire, when I follow paths that are self-created and self-directed—in fact, any time the word "self" can be used in the description of what I am doing—I am dancing to a dangerous drummer called self-love. Even things that are lauded in our society—like self-motivation, self-assertiveness, and self-development—can present deceptive stumbling blocks to one who in truth longs to "deny *himself*" (Matthew 16:24) and allow himself to be caught up within the Life of his God and King.

Now, let me ask this: If God truly loves me, will He foster and nurture within me these pervasive self-centered attitudes? Obviously not. Were He to do that, He would not be placing Himself on the controlling throne of my life. He would not be freeing me from my self-love. Instead, He would be confirming me in it.

I remember when I first put these realizations together. The clear conclusion was very distressing. You see, I at last understood that despite all the sincerity I had poured into my worship during the years I was a Protestant, God, *out of His love for me*, could not fully reveal Himself in the worship I offered Him.

Believe me, I found that a heart-rending and tearful judgment to pronounce upon myself. But its truth was inescapable. After all, God could not have been on the "throne of my life" when *I* was the one directing how He and I would relate to each other. When I picked the time, the place, and the method of worship, who was in charge—God, or me? If God had accepted such worship, He would have been establishing me in my self-centeredness. That He would not do.

I remember countering by saying to myself, "Well, I was prayerfully following the Holy Spirit's direction; so God was really the one in charge." But as we discussed earlier, verifying that *I'm* the one listening to the Spirit is a very difficult thing to do. How can I have confidence that I am being directed by the Holy Spirit when the way I worship serves to thwart the desires of the Spirit? After all, the way I choose to worship separates me from Protestant brethren who worship differently. I'm stuck with just guessing that I'm the one who's got it right. My consoling hope is that God really wishes everyone would do what I do. But what is that hope, except one more self-centered thought?

When I worshiped God in a way that was meaningful or comfortable or relevant for me, for whom was I really concerned—God, or myself? When my worship life was founded upon "Here is what I feel should be pleasing worship to You, God. Please honor it," whose will was I asking to be done—God's, or mine? So when I was the one deciding what particular acts of worship would be offered to Him, God could not fully join in them. Had He done so, He would have been capitulating to my will. The role of creature and Creator would have been reversed. God would never allow that.

Of course, when I came to grips with all this, another huge question arose before me: "Well, if in all my Protestant years God wasn't really responding to my acts of worship, *what was it* that I felt in worship?" In worship, I often felt warmth, joy, tenderness, repentance, rapture, and peace. If that wasn't God, what was it?

As Orthodox Christians, we do not believe for a moment that the work of the Holy Spirit is limited just to us. As I've shared in this book, there were times during my Protestant years when God met me as I sought Him out. There were moments when it *was* God. But I also had to admit that those particular encounters were rare, and of a nature that made them unique with respect to everything else that I called "the Presence of God." In fact, those experiences usually occurred *outside* the context of my regular worship rituals. Their real effect was to nudge me toward God by showing me that the power and beauty of a *real* relationship with Him lay far beyond the Christian life I was living.

But honesty told me that most of what I had called "the Presence of God" was really just a very natural and emotional response to my beliefs. I believed that I should be experiencing God in these ways, and so I did. People are capable of responding with great strength of emotion to ideals they hold. They die for principles. They can be stirred to the depths of their hearts by political and social causes. So it is not strange that my beliefs about my highest and greatest ideal—God—should produce the significant feelings that I believed ought to be associated with them.

Selfless Sacraments

So I concluded that the rituals of Protestant worship, no matter what their form, could not genuinely open the doorway to union and communion with God. From the liturgy of Lutheranism, to the "Spirit-filled" practices of the Pentecostals, to the down-home music and preaching of the Southern Baptists, the flaw remains: such worship is separated from the original Church, *man-created*, not *God-ordained*. Thus it can never lead to real unity, either among believers, or between believers and their God.

Now I know that if the Protestant experience is all one has ever known, the point I'm making is incredibly difficult to accept. It certainly was for me. But compare what happens in Protestant worship to what occurs in Orthodox sacramental worship. First and foremost, in Orthodox worship, self is necessarily disarmed. Consider the hymn I offer at the Liturgy, or the prayer I say before Communion, or the candle I light before an icon. I have nothing to do with creating any of these rituals. God has given them to me through His Church to practice to His glory.

God knows my weakness, my inability to tame the self-love that burns within me. That is why, in His love and wisdom, He calls me to open the door of my heart *His* way, to worship Him sacramentally. Since these sacramental acts are offered to God in simple obedience, free from my own prejudices, tastes, and designs, performing them automatically requires me to lay aside my self-will and my self-desires. There is no room for what I want—only for what Christ commands through His Holy Church.

I've had Protestant friends look at my Orthodox worship and proclaim, "Look at this ritualism. You have no freedom in your worship!" I only wish they could understand me when I tell them that being able to come to the worship of our almighty God with my independent spirit silenced and my self-centeredness in handcuffs is the most astounding freedom I could ever imagine. The incalculable blessing is, I don't have to struggle to make worship happen. As I yield my will to God's, the sacrament itself becomes my path to worship.

But that is not the only liberation an Orthodox believer experiences. When he comes to the sacrament, he is mentally and emotionally free. He does not have to decide what he will do, or why he should do it, or how he should feel about doing it, or what the results of doing it should be. He simply abandons all that, and *acts* as God directs. Thus, the obedient child finds himself caught up in the middle of an act that is from God, fulfilling Christ's prayer,

> that they all may be one, as You, Father, are in Me, and I in You; that they also may be one in Us, that the world may believe that You sent Me. And the glory which You gave Me I have given them, that they may be one just as We are one: I in them, and You in Me; that they may be made perfect in one (John 17:21–23).

All As One

Not only do the sacraments of Orthodoxy free the individual believer from self-directed worship and bind him to God, they also establish Orthodox believers in oneness. But while liturgy brings unity, there is also diversity among Orthodox people. We are not cookie-cutter Christians! For instance, within the life of prayer, individual believers have their personal practices. If there were not this freedom, we would just be robots.

Although the practice of a sacrament may differ slightly from place to place, or from person to person, the sacrament itself does not alter. How this works can be illustrated by an analogy drawn from the Classical period in Western music. Within that genre, composers had to abide by fairly strict rules of form for the pieces they created; if they did not, their works would not be popularly accepted. Yet within the boundaries of those rules, the individuality of various composers flourished. Mozart and Haydn both wrote according to the same conventions, yet they are distinctly different artists.

The sacraments are like that. That's the way they must be, given their dual role of establishing the person in a unique love relationship with God, while at the same time uniting all individual lovers of God to each other. From experience I can tell you, the sacraments accomplish both with a power and beauty that is utterly mysterious.

Imagine what it is like to know you are one with two hundred and fifty million people on this planet. We pray the very same prayers. The same hymns rise from our lips. On any particular day, at the designated hours of worship, our churches all resound with the very same services.

Here's something even more overwhelming. I am in a singular parade with all the men, women, and children who have marched this Orthodox way for two millennia before me. Following them, I see the stains of their tears, and of their blood, along the route. But ringing joyously from the head of the line to the place where I stand is the glorious song of the first Christians. And I sing *their* song, just as I say *their* prayers, and worship as *they* worshiped. Together, our hearts burn with the undying fire of the One Christ, the Head of the column.

Make no mistake. This oneness can be deeply felt and is utterly transforming. When I pray in the midst of that oneness, my heart becomes as large and as old as the Church herself. Within me there is no time, no space—just this endless procession of the millions of faithful hearts who comprise the ancient and unchanging Church. In the beauty of that wholeness, I lose myself.

But nowhere is the oneness more genuinely felt than with the people of my parish, with whom I live and worship. Sometimes on Sunday mornings, after we have all received the Body and Blood of our precious Lord Jesus Christ from a single chalice, I look into the faces of my brothers and sisters. We represent the full spectrum of human variety. Some are intellectuals; some are not. Some are rich; some live in poverty. Some are laborers; others professionals. Some struggle to read; others are always reading deeply spiritual books. Some walk among the socially elite; some are not social. Some could express the joys of their faith with eloquence; some would stumble trying to do so.

But when my eyes meet theirs, the knowledge that we are joined in a way no other human beings on earth are joined rises up in my soul. For in the very same act of obedience, we have all been touched by Christ. In calling each of us to this one sacramental act, God sets us all on level ground. Christ has given Himself equally to all. The same Spirit has placed us all within the same divine moment of unity. All our differences have become unimportant; we are truly one. This is the legacy of the unbroken Faith, the destiny of those who walk its sacramental path.

→ 11 ←

The Light and the Path

In the face of the enormously conflicting doctrines held by Bible-believing Christians, most Protestants who look at Orthodoxy seem willing to admit to the problems that scriptural interpretation causes. But to be honest, they also struggle with squaring certain Orthodox sacraments with the Bible—things like venerating icons, or making the sign of the Cross, or prayer for the departed. The problem, they will say, is that such practices don't seem to appear in the Scriptures. And if that is so, how can they be justified?

The Surprising Problem

However, a Protestant who thinks that way is begging the question. You see, before one can question a practice of the ancient Church on the basis that it is not clearly spelled out in the pages of the New Testament, one first must assume that the early Church operated on the doctrine of *sola scriptura*. (That Latin phrase, as I noted earlier in the book, means "the Bible alone," a slogan the early followers of Martin Luther used in their standoff with Rome.) But if the early Church did *not* subscribe to that doctrine, then the fact that a particular practice is not specifically described and commanded in the Scriptures does not by itself make that practice wrong.

So we must ask, did the early Church hold to *sola scriptura?* The answer is easy: it did *not*. The fact is, it could not. First of all, the Apostle Paul tells us in the Scriptures that the early Church was not committed to *sola scriptura*. He writes the Thessalonians that

> we are bound to give thanks to God always for you, brethren beloved by the Lord, because God from the beginning chose you for salvation through sanctification by the Spirit and belief in the truth, to which He called you by our

gospel, for the obtaining of the glory of our Lord Jesus Christ. Therefore, brethren, stand fast and hold the *traditions* which you were taught, whether *by word* or *our epistle* (2 Thessalonians 2:13–15, italics mine).

Thus, the Apostle makes it clear that there were traditions of doctrine and practice not communicated in writings to which Christians were nevertheless wholly obligated. Here we have the man responsible for writing the bulk of the New Testament epistles admonishing his spiritual children to observe practices that he taught them "by word," but which were not set down in his letters. Obviously, St. Paul did not see being written down as essential for a tradition to be spiritually necessary.

Secondly, we know that the Church was functioning as the pillar of truth (see 1 Timothy 3:15), worshiping God and preaching Christ to the world, for many years before the first New Testament documents were even produced. St. Paul's earliest epistles were written around AD 50. That means for nearly twenty years, the Church had no New Testament writings at all. Obviously, it *could not* have observed *sola scriptura* when there was no New Testament *scriptura!* So how on earth did the Church get along without those writings we believe to be inspired? It operated under the guidance of the Holy Spirit (concerning whom Jesus taught, "He will guide you into all truth"—John 16:13), following the traditions of the holy Apostles.

Now, when one recognizes that the Church was alive and well many years before the New Testament documents were written, one also realizes that there is absolutely no reason to view the Epistles and Gospels as exhaustive treatises on Christian doctrine and practice. In fact, the Apostle John reminds us, "And there are also many other things that Jesus did, which if they were written one by one, I suppose that even the world itself could not contain the books that would be written" (John 21:25). In their writings, the New Testament authors were addressing a thriving Church whose doctrine and rituals of worship had already been established by the Holy Spirit through the Apostles.

Thus, while inspired by the Holy Spirit and trustworthy and precious to the Church, the New Testament writings were never meant to be the complete theological guidebook that Protestant believers want them to be. In fact, it is obvious when one reads the Epistles that they were generally directed toward specific needs or problems facing either the Church at large, or some particular congregation.

The writers of the Gospels and Epistles introduced no new doctrine. Rather, they confirmed what the Apostles were already teaching and admonished the Christians to live by it. Thus, when we consider the place of the apostolic writings in the early Church, we cannot see them as an unabridged manual of good Christianity. The Gospels and Epistles were not produced to *create* or *construct* the Faith. Rather, with divine inspiration they were written to *clarify* it and to *exhort* the faithful to remain true to it.

Nothing puts the true role of the New Testament Scriptures in perspective better than the point I made in Chapter 8—that the apostolic writings don't provide much specific detail about *how* to live out the Faith. (The multitude of contradictory worship practices and lifestyles among Protestants is sufficient evidence of that, surely.) For instance, the New Testament does not even contain a detailed order of worship for Christians to follow in their services.

But amazingly, we learn from Christian writers of the second century (St. Justin and Hippolytus) that the shape of the Church's liturgy has always been essentially the same—at all times and in all places. How is this possible, without a New Testament directive? It's simple. The "hows" of worship—like the order of service in the liturgy—did not need to be explained in the New Testament writings, because they had already been firmly established in the life of the Church by the Apostles and their followers. In that light, we can see that the real purpose of the New Testament writings was to keep Christians moving straight ahead on the path that had been set before them by the Holy Spirit through the Apostles—years before those Gospels and Epistles were ever penned.

As the Church went forward into new lands, the New Testament writings provided a divine tool for spreading the message of

Christ and instructing and edifying the faithful. But even then, the relationship of the Scriptures and Tradition remained the same. The written Word set forth the essential beliefs of the Faith. This Word opened men's hearts to Jesus Christ. As they emerged from the waters of baptism, these new believers entered into the daily life of Christ and His Holy Church. And that daily life was defined by the same practices of Holy Tradition that had guided the Church from apostolic times.

The Scriptures: "A Light Unto My Path"

So the ancient Church looks back at those first days of the Faith and sees the apostolic writings as a great diamond, the centerpiece of a majestic crown, set among other precious stones. The surrounding gems include the practices of liturgical worship and other elements that we call Holy Tradition.

What, then, is the difference in the way an Orthodox Christian and a Protestant believer treat the New Testament Scriptures? To borrow an old and often-recited simile, a Protestant believer approaches the Scriptures like a gold mine. Using every tool at his disposal (the original languages, commentaries, concordances), he digs into the rich recesses of this mine. He searches for nuggets of spiritual wisdom, and when he finds one, he applies it to his spiritual life. Thus, any tradition of worship that he would find acceptable would have to be excavated from that mine.

But an Orthodox Christian's relationship to the Scriptures goes deeper than the Protestant's. For an Orthodox Christian does not see the Word of God as a gold mine to be worked. After all, the Church, the Kingdom, is the repository of gold. Thus, he sees the Scriptures more as a light that illumines faith and worship. He sings the Scriptures. He prays the Scriptures. In his worship, he even kisses the Scriptures. They are the constant light of his life. He measures time and seasons by them. Yet in contrast to the image of the laboring miner, he does all this as gently and naturally as one who stands in the warmth of a bright, clear spring morning, inhaling its fresh and glorious fragrance.

As paradoxical as it may seem to the Protestant, in the two

thousand years since Pentecost, Orthodoxy has never embraced *sola scriptura*—or *sola* anything! There has been no reason to do so. For the Scriptures, the hymns, the sacraments, the icons, the laity, and the clergy all form a beautifully woven tapestry of faith and life in Christ.

Let me illustrate. Consider that well-known text from the Psalms: "Your word is a lamp to my feet / And a light to my path" (Psalm 119:105). If a Protestant thinks carefully, he will recognize that this verse does not accurately depict his *sola scriptura* version of the Christian life. For to the Protestant, the Word is *everything*. The "lamp," the "light," and the "path" aren't really different things, because they are all found *in and through the Word*.

I ask my Protestant reader to ponder upon each of those three words for a moment. As a Protestant, I looked into the *light* of the Word often. Even when it came to figuring out the *path* I should walk—that is, when it came to identifying the things I should *do*—I looked into the Word.

But my path never seemed very plain. Like most of the devoted believers I knew, I seemed to be constantly looking for it. "Where do you want me to step now, God?" was the question I asked, day in and day out. I usually tried to respond to that question by studying the Word. But sometimes, I looked to other things. I would pray for signs. Sometimes I'd try new twists and turns in my prayer and worship life, all in an ongoing effort to find the path God wanted me to walk.

But for the Orthodox Christian, the psalmist's dual elements of light (or lamp) and pathway make perfect sense. The light and the path are distinctly different things to him. On one hand, an Orthodox Christian has a clear, God-ordained *path*. It is Holy Tradition—the way of belief, worship, and sacramental life that the Apostles gave to the Church even before the New Testament was written. Because he has this, the devout Orthodox believer can rise every morning with a clear picture of how and where he must walk that day. He knows there are specific spiritual tasks that he must perform. Surprises and unforeseen events are taken in stride. They don't throw him off the track.

But the world through which his path cuts its course is a sin-stained one. The Orthodox believer knows that he could never stay on that path, were it not for the blessed *light* that illumines it. The Scriptures are that lamp and light.

So, although both are critical elements of the journey, Orthodox Christians sharply differentiate between the light that shines above the path (the Scriptures), and the path itself (Apostolic Tradition). For the path by itself cannot show us its destination, or give us reason to walk it. Nor can the light that illumines the way provide the solid earth on which we may confidently tread. Both are required, and both are the gifts of God. So for Orthodox Christians, the Bible and Tradition are dear friends, not enemies!

This hand-in-hand relationship of Scripture and Tradition brings crystalline clarity to the Orthodox Christian's life. He doesn't have to labor furiously to understand Scripture, because its meaning is already reflected by the Tradition it illuminates and nourishes. (Though to be candid, some of us Orthodox believers need to know the Scriptures far better than we do.) And he has confidence in the Tradition of the Faith, because he sees it clearly by the lamp and light of the Holy Scriptures.

The Leading of the Spirit

Actually, if the Protestant believer stops and reflects upon his own experience for a moment, he will realize that he has his own extrabiblical traditions. It is commonplace for him to observe spiritual practices and to heed spiritual commandments not found in the Scriptures. These things he does just as faithfully as the things he can back up by quoting chapter and verse.

I wonder how many millions of Protestant brethren have claimed, "The Holy Spirit led me" to do something? Most have, I'm sure. Maybe it was to bear witness to someone in a restaurant, or call someone on the phone, or send some money to someone, or not get on a plane, or one of a thousand other possible scenarios.

This same "leading of the Spirit" would be appealed to if I asked questions about the different worship practices to which various Protestants adhere. Why do some pastors strictly follow an expository method, while others always do topical sermons? Why do some churches have altar calls every week, while others have them rarely? Why do some churches have full worship bands and sing nothing but choruses, while others use hymns and organs? Why do some have communion every month, while others do it weekly or quarterly? Why do some congregations have children's church, while others make the little ones sit through the sermons like everyone else?

In every case, personal or corporate, the answer would be, "This is what we have been directed by the Holy Spirit to do!" So what would the typical Protestant say if I asked him to show me the Scripture verse that says, "You must witness to the person at the table on your left," or "In worship, you need to sing two fast songs for every slow one"? Or what if I asked, "Where does the Bible teach that we need a Sunday school?"

He'd probably smile at me and reply, "You obviously understand nothing about the leading of the Holy Spirit! For the Spirit of God inspires us to lots of actions that are not specifically spelled out in the Bible."

So here's my question: If it is normal for the contemporary Protestant to experience real direction of the Holy Spirit outside of the Scriptures, *why should the same not have been true for the early Church?* Why does the Protestant assume that he (or his church, or his denomination) can be guided in such a way, but that the Holy Spirit could not have inspired the early Church in that way? Why shouldn't the Holy Tradition of the ancient Church be seen in the same way— as the inspired activity of the Holy Spirit outside the specific writings of the New Testament?

Of course, that Protestant would insist that his extrabiblical activities are in accord with the Scriptures. But many Orthodox practices, he would urge, are completely inconsistent with the teachings of the Scriptures. And certainly, there was a time when I myself would have adamantly proclaimed that same thing. But that was before I looked at myself in the mirror and asked, "How do I know that?"

It was a great awakening for me finally to realize that labeling such practices as unscriptural was, from my Protestant position, a completely empty claim. For as a Protestant, what was I really saying when I declared that? It was this: "These things cannot be right because they are incompatible with my interpretation of the Scriptures, and my belief that truth is determined by the Scriptures alone—which, of course, are the very same convictions that lead me and my Protestant brethren to hold contradictory beliefs on every important matter of faith, and splinter Protestantism into thousands of factions."

It dawned on me that if I was going to call the Christians of the early centuries heretics because they did not act in accordance with *my* understanding of the Scriptures, then I should be calling the bulk of my Protestant brethren heretics as well. But that would get me nowhere in my search for truth. I realized that I needed some other frame of reference to help me judge the practices of the ancient Faith.

I found that frame of reference when I finally realized that the New Testament Scriptures had been delivered to a Church that already had established traditions of doctrine and worship. Determining what was scriptural or unscriptural, then, took on an entirely different complexion. For I saw that to understand what the *words* of the New Testament documents actually meant to the people to whom they were written, one must understand the *traditions* that formed the context in which those words were received.

When I began to look at things that way, I was astounded. But I was also saddened. For I discovered that by focusing on the *words* of the New Testament, without knowing—sometimes even denying—the context of the traditions in which they were written, I had all my life cut myself off from any hope of knowing Christianity as the first Christians knew it. Without understanding those traditions, all I could ever know was a partial expression of that Faith.

A Case in Point

Let me expand this point by showing how some early Christian leaders saw as completely compatible with the Scriptures a tradition that absolutely appalls many evangelical Protestants. The issue is infant baptism. As a Protestant, I'd always been told that this is an unbiblical practice that began to surface around the fourth century. I was assured that the early Church's view on baptism was the same as any good evangelical's: baptism is the public declaration of a person's rational choice to repent and follow Christ. After all, that's what the Scriptures say in Acts 2:38: "Repent, and . . . be baptized." Since infants aren't capable of such a choice, infant baptism is wrong.

But when I was researching my master's thesis in philosophy, I began for the first time to read early Church literature for myself, including the writings of St. Irenaeus (130–202). Irenaeus received the Faith from St. Polycarp, who himself had been led to Christ by the beloved Apostle John. From his words, it is clear that Irenaeus saw the salvation of infants as being as much a part of Christ's work as His saving of adults. In his *Against Heresies*, Irenaeus writes:

For He [Christ] came to save all through means of Himself—*all*, I say, who through Him are *born again* to God—*infants*, and children, and boys, and youths, and old men. He therefore passed through every age, *becoming an infant for infants, thus sanctifying infants*; a child for children, thus sanctifying those who are of this age, being at the same time made to them as an example of piety, righteousness, and submission (italics mine).[1]

If an infant can be "born again," should he be denied baptism? The early Church held that he should not. Writing just a few years after Irenaeus, Origen (182–251) says:

Could a child who has only just been born commit a sin? And yet he has sin for which it is commanded to offer a sacrifice, as Job 14:4 and Psalm 51:5–7 show. For this reason the Church *received from the Apostles* the tradition to administer baptism to children also. For the men to whom the secrets of divine mysteries had been entrusted knew that in everyone there were genuine sinful defilements, which had to be washed away with water and the Spirit (italics mine).[2]

In the early 200s, a council of bishops was called to consider whether the baptism of male infants should be delayed until after circumcision had been performed. Writing on behalf of that council, St. Cyprian (200–258), later martyred for the cause of Christ, set down these words:

> We all rather judge that the mercy and grace of God is not to be refused to anyone born of man . . . no one is to be hindered from obtaining grace by that law which was already ordained, and that spiritual circumcision [referring to baptism] ought not to be hindered . . . no one ought to be hindered from baptism and from the grace of God, who is merciful and kind and loving to all. *Which, since it is to be observed and maintained in respect of all, we think is to be even more observed in respect of infants and newly-born persons,* who on this very account deserve more from our help and from the divine mercy (italics mine).[3]

Now remember, I was a Protestant when I first read these things. They disturbed me greatly. Here were these writings (and there are more), all before the fourth century, which supported the practice of infant baptism. *Nowhere* could I find an early Church writer who condemned it.

I also learned that all these men—Irenaeus, Origen, Cyprian, and the others—revered the Book of Acts as inspired by God. So they saw their belief about the salvation and baptism of infants as completely compatible with Acts 2:38. *How could that possibly be?* I thought.

Of course, when I was a Protestant, I simply would have assumed men who taught such "unscriptural" things were just plain wrong—maybe even wolves in sheep's clothing. They were just like all the rest of those early Church leaders whose obvious goal was to pervert the true Faith. How could I be sure of this? Why, because of *sola scriptura,* of course.

I must confess that I have spent many tearful moments on my knees before God, begging forgiveness for having slandered the character of His blessed servants—all in the name of a slogan that did not exist for the first fifteen hundred years of Church history, an innovation that has served to divide and confuse God's people in their attempts to know Him.

Maybe It Is Scriptural

Once I had gotten free of my *sola scriptura* biases, I actually began to see that things like infant baptism weren't unscriptural at all. Given a fair hearing, these practices show themselves to be perfectly consistent with the Scriptures.

So then, how do the Scriptures bear witness to the sacraments of the Church—specifically, that baptism is also for infants? Join me in the next chapter for the answer.

Part III

The Way of Love

✦ 12 ✦

It's Not Just for Grown-Ups Anymore!

Scriptural Precedent

One way of looking at the scriptural consistency of infant baptism is to consider this: If the Apostles themselves were to have appealed to Scripture for guidance about infant baptism, what help would they have found? Of course, we must remember that the only Scriptures the Apostles had to work with at the start were the books of the Old Testament. What light would these have shed on the issue?

Let us imagine the Apostles going forth after Pentecost, fulfilling Christ's commission to preach the Gospel and baptize those who were converted by it. What if one of those converts, someone like the jailer in Acts 16, had asked the Apostles, "Can my six-month-old daughter also receive baptism?" To what scriptural guidance could they have turned for the answer?

Well, the writings of the Apostles that became the New Testament clearly teach us that they saw baptism as the sign of a New Covenant relationship with Christ. In baptism, we are buried with Christ and raised with Him in the power of the Holy Spirit. Every covenant God has ever made with men has had its visible sign. In His covenant with Israel, God's sign was circumcision. Without question, the Apostles would have concurred with St. Cyprian's description of baptism as "spiritual circumcision."

So the question the Apostles would have asked, as they looked for guidance on infant baptism, was, "What do the Scriptures teach us about who can be included in God's Covenant and receive its sign?" As Jews, the absolute, one-hundred-percent scriptural answer would have been obvious to them.

You see, in the case of the Old Covenant, God did not just *allow* infants to receive its sign of circumcision. He *commanded* it to be given at eight days of age to every boy born to the house of Israel. This would seem to be straightforward scriptural evidence for baptizing infants.

The Spirit's Indwelling

A Protestant response to this might be, "But we're not talking about the Old Covenant here. We're talking about the New." Now, I must say that I question the merits of arguing that the God of ineffable mercy and unfathomable love would gladly bestow the blessings of the covenant of law upon infants, yet would refuse them initiation into His covenant of grace. But I am willing to examine the question from a purely New Testament standpoint. We shall see, though, that the apostolic writings yield the same conclusion: Infant baptism is thoroughly consistent with the teachings of the Scriptures (Old Testament and New).

As a Protestant, the text to which I always pointed to protest the idea of infant baptism was, of course, Acts 2:38: "Then Peter said to them, 'Repent, and let every one of you be baptized in the name of Jesus Christ for the remission of sins.'"

That's where I typically stopped reading. To me, that seemed enough to prove to anyone that in order to be baptized, repentance is required. Babies cannot repent. It's as simple as that. But as I began to look into this question in earnest, I realized that the passage goes further. Reading the entire verse, plus the one after it, forces one to take a broader look at things:

Then Peter said to them, "Repent, and let every one of you be baptized in the name of Jesus Christ for the remission of sins; *and you shall receive the gift of the Holy Spirit.* For *the promise* is to you and to your *children*, and to all who are afar off, as many as the Lord our God will call" (Acts 2:38, 39; italics mine).

There are a number of important things to see here. First, baptism is not the final goal of repentance. The purpose of repentance and baptism is to bestow upon the believer the gift of the Holy

Spirit. The Holy Spirit is the "promise" of which Peter speaks here (see Acts 2:33). Peter declares that the gift of the indwelling Spirit is also for the *children* of those who are listening to his words.

Here again is the ancient Church's understanding of salvation as a *living process*. Repentance and baptism, Peter teaches, are steps toward the ultimate goal of Christian Faith: finding God living within us. His indwelling is the identifying mark of a true Christian, the "guarantee" that we are Christ's "purchased possession" (Ephesians 1:14).

This is vividly corroborated a little later in the Book of Acts. In Chapter 8, we see Peter and John going down to Samaria. They find believers there who have been baptized in the name of Jesus. But the final step, the coming of the Holy Spirit upon them, has not yet occurred. To the Apostles, this is an unacceptable situation, and they rectify it immediately. The lives of these believers would not be complete until the whole process—repentance, baptism, *and* the indwelling of the Holy Spirit—had been manifested.

How does this all relate to infant baptism? The story of the Samaritan Christians tells us that it is not the ability to repent and be baptized that ultimately shows one to be a Christian. Repenting and being baptized are not the final steps in following Christ. The process must include *the indwelling of the Spirit*.

Thus the real issue that must be discussed, when it comes to infants, is not, "Can babies repent?" Rather, it is, "Can the Spirit of God dwell within infants?" If the answer is "Yes," then on the authority of the Scriptures and the Apostle Peter, we must baptize babies.

This is made clear in the story of Cornelius and his household (Acts 10). As St. Peter preached to them, the Holy Spirit fell on them. Now, since Cornelius had gathered all his relatives and good friends to hear Peter (v. 24), and since the Holy Spirit fell on everyone in the house (v. 44), it is most likely that the Spirit fell on some young children—probably even infants.

But for the sake of argument, let's assume all in attendance were adults. Here were people upon whom the Holy Spirit had just descended, but who as yet had not been baptized in water. When the question arose about whether or not they should be baptized, St. Peter declared: "Can anyone forbid water, that these should not be baptized who have received the Holy Spirit just as we have?" (Acts 10:47). In the mind of St. Peter, baptism and the Spirit's presence are inseparable, like two acts of the same play. If the *seal* of the New Covenant (the Holy Spirit) is present in someone, the *sign* of that Covenant (baptism) must certainly be bestowed upon him—whether he's eighty years old or eight days old.

So let us ask: "Can the Spirit of God reside within infants and small children?" How would a Protestant answer this question? Were I to ask, "Do infants need to be saved?" most Protestants would reply, "Yes." They recognize that no one is born without the stain of sin, except One. Does God want to save infants? "Of course," they would answer. Did Christ die to save them? Again, the answer would be emphatically, "Yes."

But things change when the question is, "Does Christ want His Spirit to indwell an infant?" We have just seen that St. Peter's teaching and practice is that baptism and the indwelling of the Holy Spirit are related. So, in the light of the Scriptures, the only logically consistent answer that an evangelical Protestant who forbids infant baptism can give is, "No, the Spirit cannot indwell the infant." Why? He believes that the child cannot be baptized until he reaches the "age of accountability" (which, curiously, is a concept mentioned absolutely nowhere in the Scriptures!). A young person must first recognize his need for God, repent, and confess his belief in Christ. Only then can he or she be baptized as a public announcement of his or her inward commitment to God. Only then, from the Protestant view, can the Spirit of God indwell that young person.

A Self-Contradicting Belief

My problems with infant baptism began to disappear as I started to examine carefully the implications of my evangelical viewpoint. Some of them were absolutely devastating. For instance, I realized that to declare infant baptism wrong actually forced me to deny one of the most fundamental tenets of my Protestant faith!

How so? Well, as a Protestant, I was not only committed to *sola scriptura.* I was also committed to the doctrine that salvation is by grace alone, *sola gratia.* But my belief that children cannot be baptized until they reach the "age of accountability" plainly showed that I did not believe in salvation by grace *alone.* For I obviously believed that a child's redemption ultimately hinges not upon grace, but upon his ability to understand the plan of salvation. No matter how much the Holy Spirit may want to bestow grace on that child, He must hover in a holding pattern about the child's soul until he or she reaches a certain intellectual level. So in my Protestant view, I realized that I actually believed in "salvation through human understanding *and* grace," not *sola gratia.*

But then, I raised this objection to myself: "No. Even though he must reach an age where he can intellectually understand salvation before he can receive it, a child's salvation is still founded solely upon grace. For it is God's grace that leads the child to understand His need for God, to exercise faith, and to confess Christ."

This changes nothing, however. For if this is the case, it is still apparent that for a long time in the child's life, grace *is* present, while salvation is *not.* Obviously, then, it takes something *more* than grace to bring about the child's redemption. To be true to my Protestant theology, I had to believe that until children reach that level of intellect that allows them to understand their plight as sinners and confess faith in Christ, infants and children stand outside the reach of God's salvation. The oddity of that implication struck me powerfully when I thought about the fact that Jesus declares these little ones to be the true recipients of the Kingdom of God (Luke 18:16)!

To this, however, I raised an old and common protest: "Look, God makes a provision for infants and young children. He knows that at their age, they can't understand their need for salvation. So if they die in that state, God will not condemn them."

That's something I myself preached from the pulpit probably dozens of times. But as I made my way toward Orthodoxy, I began to see the rather morbid implications of what I'd taught all those years. What I had declared, essentially, was that an infant or young child cannot know the indwelling Spirit of God in his life unless he dies! If he *dies*, he is wrapped in the loving embrace of God's presence. But if he *lives*, he's stuck in a spiritual limbo, where both he and God await the day when he at last becomes intelligent enough to recognize that he needs Christ!

It finally dawned on me that I'd had a very grim view of the spiritual aspects of infancy and childhood. I ultimately had to confront myself with this thought: Can this possibly be the picture of children that Jesus had in His heart when they brought infants to Him and He said, "Let the little children come to Me, and do not forbid them; for of such is the kingdom of God"? (Luke 18:15, 16).

Now, I remember getting very exasperated with the realities that confronted me at that point. All these necessary ramifications of my Protestant attitude toward infant baptism were completely unacceptable to me. I found them entirely inconsistent with Christ's admonition that "unless you are converted and become as little children, you will by no means enter the kingdom of heaven" (Matthew 18:3).

So at last I insisted to myself: "I believe the Spirit of God does indwell little children. But the ability to repent is the only real evidence we have that the Spirit of God is working in the child. Thus, we can't acknowledge that presence of the Spirit by baptism until the child reaches the age where he accepts responsibility for his acts and repents. Babies can't do that."

But, I reasoned, maybe Jesus was looking at something besides just repentance when He declared little children to be heaven's model citizens. What of the meekness, humility, and simple faith that we see in the very young? Are these not evidence of God's influence? I myself have been humbled to tears by the Spirit of God speaking through a little child on more than one occasion. I cannot imagine that most other Protestants have not had similar experiences.

So I faced the fact that the Spirit of God can be found in the hearts of children. But in that declaration, I'd come full circle, and saw myself completely at odds with the teaching of St. Peter: "Can anyone forbid water, that these should not be baptized who have received the Holy Spirit just as we have?" (Acts 10:47). At last, I understood that I must be all for baptizing children. For the teaching of the New Testament is that baptism and the Spirit's indwelling are inseparable. The examples of St. Peter's sermon on Pentecost, the Samaritan Christians, and Cornelius's household all make it clear that if one is present, the other must be.

What about Free Will?

Of course, someone might still object, "Well, maybe baptizing young children is okay. But infants? What about free will? It might be one thing to baptize a young child. But to baptize an infant who cannot even consciously choose Christ is akin to forcing salvation on him. The child's free will has been compromised. God does not do that."

The fact is, an infant's total inability to make a free-will decision with regard to God is the ultimate argument *for* infant baptism (recall the quote in the last chapter from St. Cyprian). Infants, to be sure, do not choose what sorts of forces will play about in their hearts and souls. They are the most spiritually vulnerable of all creatures. Do you suppose the devil has any reluctance about moving into the heart of an infant to work his terrible schemes upon that innocent one? Would the God of Love leave the children of His beloved ones to that terrible fate?

The obvious truth is, He never would, and He never has. God does not leave innocents out there in limbo, fair game for every evil spirit that comes along. Because of their weakness, He has always given infants His utmost protection. That's why He placed His sign on Israelite babies—to bring them under the full protective covering of His Covenant. In this, He declared to Satan that these little ones were not fair game.

Under the New Covenant, God does the same thing. The Apostles and early Christians knew that. That's why they baptized their babies. By this act, they faithfully opened the souls of their children to the Holy Spirit, allowing Him to take up His protective residence within them. And interestingly, in the Orthodox baptismal liturgy, the priest first casts out any possible lurking influence of the devil before the child is joined to Christ in baptism.

But there is another important reason why God would take up residence in the lives of these infants. You see, unless He does, the child will never have the real opportunity to decide for himself whether or not he will follow God. Why do I say that? Well, if the Holy Spirit does not take up residence in the infant, guess who will. Does Satan give those whom he afflicts a free choice? Hardly. No, the only one who would ever allow a child to have free choice when it comes to following or rejecting Christ is Christ Himself.

The ancient Faith recognizes there will come a day in a child's life when he reaches an intellectual or moral crossroad. We might even call it an age of accountability. He will recognize as never before that he often strays from the path of Christ. Before him, he will see in a new, mature way the demands of the pathway, and the consequences of departing from it. As never before, he will know that he stands personally and eternally responsible to God for his actions. Every child—Protestant, Roman Catholic, or Orthodox—faces that moment.

But that day dawns much differently for the Orthodox child than for the young Protestant. As the Orthodox youngster faces it, he has the assurance that God the Father loves him, and that the Lord Jesus Christ has lived in him since birth. He has been baptized. He has received the Holy Spirit. From infancy, he has partaken of the Body and Blood of Christ through the Eucharist. His parents, his teachers, his priest, his entire community—everyone in his life has nurtured him in the knowledge that he is wholly God's.

So when that day of new awareness comes, the Orthodox child knows that he has always been a child of the redeeming God—a fully vested member of the Body of Christ. He must make his awesome choice. But the choice he faces is whether or not he shall *continue* to live in the blessed relationship with God that has always been his.

Repentance
The issue of infant baptism was one of the most heart-rending of all the confrontations I had with myself as I began to study early Church teachings. There have been many times when I have shed tears of repentance and regret for things I once believed, and more regrettably, once taught. But this issue hit me especially hard on that

personal level. In it, I saw just how insidious and far-reaching the damage done by a rationalistic devotion to *sola scriptura* can be.

Look at what "by Scripture alone" and my rationalism had forced me into here. First, it made me deny everything that Jesus had to say about children. I had tacitly taken exception with my Lord, insisting that He should have said to children, "Unless you become as *adults,* you will by no means enter the kingdom of heaven."

Secondly, *sola scriptura* and my Protestant rationalism demanded that I deny everything my heart told me about children. We always talk about childlike faith. We see it in the faces of children when they talk so matter-of-factly about Christ. In their prayers, we hear a simplicity and an unwavering confidence that puts our sophisticated adult faith to shame. In a child's love for Jesus, there is no pretence. It is pure and honest. But in spite of what I knew in my heart, my doctrine required me to maintain that a child's relationship with Christ is somehow not yet genuine.

Above all, I came to the heartbreaking conclusion that as an evangelical Protestant pastor, I had corrupted the holy rite of Baptism. I had turned the holy Sacrament into an initiation rite for rationalists.

How I wish I could communicate to everyone I ever baptized that, in the ancient and True Faith, things are much different. God is not in the shadows. He is *constantly* pressing with divine force upon the soul—whether that soul is fifty years old or fifty minutes old. For Christ has purchased every soul, and jealously wants to possess every one right now. His plans for taking up residence in a soul contain no stipulations whatsoever about age or intellectual ability.

How I wish that everyone I ever baptized could see that intellectual rationalism is the seat of self-love and pride. Thus, it cannot possibly be God's chief ally; rather, it is His chief obstacle. That's why the Protestant idea that God would require us to discover Him through painstaking mental effort was completely foreign to the Apostles and early Christians—and to Israel of old.

I long for all those whom I led to Christ to know that we can have a relationship with God that exceeds anything they ever heard from me. More than that, experiencing that divine love is a completely uncomplicated process. It demands no special intellectual prowess. One just lives the vision of the Orthodox Faith. He comes to the sacraments of the Church, and by his performance of those sacramental *acts*—not words, or intellectual exercises, but *acts*—he simply presents his lost and sinful soul to his Redeemer.

You know what? When it comes to important sacraments—particularly the Eucharist—even an infant can do that! Regardless of who it is, infant or adult, Christ requires nothing more than that. Immediately He sweeps through the door that has been obediently opened and touches the soul with the beauty of His divine Presence.

In the light of that beautiful, simple, and humble Faith, I at last came to understand that infant baptism makes perfect scriptural sense. How does Jesus define *conversion*? To Him, it means "to become as a child." Why, then, does Peter tell his hearers on the Day of Pentecost that they must repent? They must do so in order to humble themselves, and *become as little children* (see Matthew 18:3, 4).

So, what does a child need to do to be converted—that is, to become as a child? Nothing, obviously—he's already there! The child, especially the infant, has already reached the goal that the adult must attain through repentance. No one is more humble or submissive toward God than this little one. Thus, according to Christ, no one is more ideally suited for baptism and the Spirit's indwelling than an infant.

Seeing with New Eyes

It didn't take long, once I began to study the sacramental life of the Church, for me to realize how much spiritual beauty I had missed in not being Orthodox. So many things had escaped my comprehension, just because I read the Scriptures in an intellectual vacuum that bound me to the letter of the New Testament. When I began to examine the historic Faith with my heart, instead of just my mind, I was amazed. Those sacramental rituals that a short time before I would have denounced, I began to see as expressions of a pure, reverent, obedient, thankful, broken-hearted, repentant, faithful, heartfelt, Spirit-filled Love. And all of them are completely consistent with the Spirit who inspires the pages of the New Testament. There was nothing wrong with my New Testament, to be sure. The problem was with me.

I've learned by experience that the Church's sacramental acts are vessels that the Spirit has put in the hands of God's people to capture and hold the love and grace that pour forth from His Holy Word. From these we drink. Thus, to me as an Orthodox Christian, the Gospels and the Epistles are more than words, more than powerful ideas. Through sacramental ritual, their words become concrete and living realities, which reach into every corner of my being.

✣ 13 ✦

The Eucharist

N othing showed me just how constricted my evangelical view of the Scriptures had been more than the subject of Communion. I had always criticized the belief, held by sacramental Christian communities, that in the Eucharist, the bread and wine actually *become* the Body and Blood of the Lord Jesus Christ. Surely, it was clear that the bread and wine could not be the *real* Body and Blood of Christ. These elements only served as symbols by which we remember His sacrifice. But in wrestling with this question, I ended up seeing I'd been wrong. More alarmingly, I came to see that my commitment to rationalism sometimes had taken precedent even over the Scriptures when it came to deciding what to believe.

I should first make something clear. Unlike Roman Catholicism, Orthodoxy has no doctrine of transubstantiation. This is the Roman doctrine that seeks to explain on a physical level *how* the bread and wine become the Body and Blood of Jesus. Interestingly enough, this doctrine was developed in response to twelfth-century rationalists who were demanding a logical explanation of the change. In Orthodoxy, we simply accept the mystery. By an unfathomable act of God, the Eucharist is bread and wine, and at the same time it is truly the Body and Blood of Christ.

How can we believe that? Because Jesus said it:

And as they were eating, Jesus took bread, blessed and broke it, and gave it to the disciples and said, "Take, eat; this is My body." Then He took the cup, and gave thanks, and gave it to them, saying, "Drink from it, all of you. For this is My blood of the new covenant, which is shed for many for the remission of sins" (Matthew 26:26–28).

And so does St. Paul:

> The cup of blessing which we bless, is it not the commun-
> ion of the blood of Christ? The bread which we break, is it
> not the communion of the body of Christ (1 Corinthians
> 10:16)?

Taking Things Literally

A Protestant who wanted to challenge my literal interpretation of
these passages could point out that Jesus uses all kinds of symbolic
language in relation to Himself. For instance, He says, "I am the
door" (John 10:7). So a critic might ask, "Does that mean He's a
seven-foot oak slab?" Of course not.

There's a difference here, of course. After all, the entire pre-
Reformation Church held the consecrated bread and wine of which
it partook each Sunday to be Christ's actual Body and Blood.
On the other hand, no one, not even the heretics, ever believed
Jesus to be a literal door. But the real question this analogy raises
is, "How do I tell whether a particular bit of biblical imagery is
meant to be taken literally or figuratively?" Protestants know that
making such determinations is a critical aspect of biblical
intepretation.

In the specific case of the Eucharist, this question becomes:
"What is the reason for determining that this particular scripture—
Jesus' reference to the bread and wine as His Body and Blood—is
one of those which must be taken figuratively? Is there any scriptural reference at all that tells me it must not be interpreted the way
the Church always has done?"

When I forced myself into that corner, I had no answer. For all
my preaching of *sola scriptura*, there was nothing whatsoever in the
Scriptures to which I could point. The only response I could muster to that question was, "It just doesn't make sense to think that
bread and wine—even by the Holy Spirit—could be Jesus' Body
and Blood. No reasonable person could accept that idea. Only some
primitive, superstitious person could possibly believe it." My own
reaction showed me my belief was not founded on the Scriptures at

all! It was built entirely on the limitations of my modern rational mind.

Living the Incarnation
As I've noted, my rationalist view was out of line with the faith of the early Church. Just after the close of the first century, St. Ignatius, who was ordained the third bishop of Antioch in AD 69, wrote a letter attacking the Docetists, one of Christianity's first heretical groups. The Docetists were proclaiming a more "spiritualized" Christianity, one that denied concrete realities of the faith. For instance, practical matters like love and care for others were not a high priority for them. What was one of their most heretical beliefs? Ignatius writes,

> But consider those who are of a different opinion with respect to the grace of Christ which has come to us, how opposed they are to the will of God. They have no regard for love; no care for the widow, or the orphan, or the oppressed; of the bond, or of the free; of the hungry, or of the thirsty. *They abstain from the Eucharist and from prayer, because they confess not the Eucharist to be the flesh of our Saviour Jesus Christ, which suffered for our sins,* and which the Father, of his goodness raised up again. . . . It is fitting, therefore, that ye should keep aloof from such persons . . . but to give heed to the Gospel, in which the passion [of Christ] has been revealed to us, and the resurrection has been fully proved (italics mine).[1]

St. Ignatius of Antioch lived during the time of the Apostles. He was the arch-shepherd of no less than the very Church that sent out Paul and Barnabas on their first missionary journey (Acts 13:2). As a bishop, he upheld the faith there for at least forty years, in the face of some of the greatest persecution the Church has ever known. He himself was martyred, torn apart by wild beasts in the Roman arena.

This man of God, versed in the Scriptures, says the Gospel

teaches us the Eucharist is the flesh of Christ. Jesus and St. Paul said it, first-century Christians believed it, and Orthodox Christians across twenty centuries have continued to believe it. I find that a far more compelling argument than the skeptical insistence of my modern rationalism that it just can't be.

Furthermore, I began to see that my resistance to the sacramental view of the Eucharist was self-contradicting. After all, how could I profess belief in something as impossible to understand as the Incarnation, and yet deny that the real Presence of Christ can be in the bread and wine of the Eucharist? Tell me: If God can be truly present within human blood and tissue, why can He not be truly present within bread and wine? After all, they are both organic matter. The molecules just have a different arrangement.

To this, though, I raised another Protestant reply: "A human form has intelligence. God could reside in that. But bread and wine are inanimate." But wait a minute! Is God prevented from placing Himself within things that are inanimate? He has spoken to us from clouds and burning bushes. Of the rock in the wilderness, St. Paul asserts, "that Rock was Christ" (1 Corinthians 10:4). I finally admitted that His omnipresent love and power allow God to place Himself anywhere He desires.

And why would He not offer to us the essential physical elements of His own human life? Jesus is not some Gnostic philosopher who redeems us by elevating our thinking, by giving us holy principles to ponder. No, He does something extremely radical—and extremely physical. He renews us by taking on our flesh-and-blood reality. God joins Himself to us, purifying our nature in His own Body, eternally binding human nature to the divine. Christ then calls us to be "partakers of the divine nature" (2 Peter 1:4), that we may be "transformed" into His likeness (2 Corinthians 3:18). Is it so odd to think that Jesus would offer to us, in a real way, the elements of His own sanctified humanity—the very humanity into which we are to be transformed?

The Taste of Life
So as an Orthodox Christian, I know my salvation comes through

living in union with Christ—now and ever and unto the ages of ages. It is a matter of allowing my God and King to draw me into His life through the sacraments of the Church—not in some distant future, but *right now*.

I imagine the Apostles, in those days after Christ ascended, celebrating the Eucharist. How did they approach this event? As a Protestant rationalist, I would have pictured them thinking, "Oh, wasn't that a glorious thing that He did back then!"

But as an Orthodox Christian, I have another sense of their thoughts: *There is only One Life in the universe who really matters. And to be with Him is all that we desire.* Of course, they had known the living, personal presence of the Son of God in His flesh. The Ascension that parted him from them must have been very difficult for the Apostles. But Christ, in His mercy, had made them a promise: "He who eats my flesh and drinks My blood abides in Me, and I in him" (John 6:56).

What joy it must have been for them to know that each time they took the holy bread and wine to their lips, He was there. Not as a memory, or a dream, or a flight of fantasy, but in the Flesh and Blood of His pure Body. The Apostles didn't have to imagine that Jesus was there in those Holy Gifts. For when Christ is present, the heart of one who loves Him knows it—in a way that the mind alone cannot fathom.

Jesus understands that we all need *Him*—not just a *memory* of Him. Our lives are so much more than thoughts and memories. God wants to redeem every part of our lives. He wants to touch every aspect of our humanity. So Christ Himself comes to us in the Eucharist, in physical gifts that touch our lips and enter our inward parts. Christ thus unites Himself with our flesh, as well as with our hearts and minds. Each time we partake of Him, we reaffirm our faith in the Incarnation, the Cross, and the Resurrection—not merely by remembering Him, but by experiencing Him. This we do, week after week, in a holy sacrament of love that establishes a concrete, constant, and undeniable interconnection with Christ our God.

What solidity it gives to one's faith, in those times when doubts assail, to be able to point to the Eucharist and say, "I know Jesus is with me, for I have received His very Body and Blood." As one who once believed himself beyond the need for tangible manifestations of the Son of God, I now joyously know myself to be a frail and simple man in need of the Master's literal touch. Thus, I am humbled beyond words before the chalice of the Holy Eucharist. There, our Lord and Master Christ bestows upon this most unworthy man the most incomprehensibly intimate Gift in all the universe—Himself. This is infinite Love.

→ 14 ←

Liturgy

There's no doubt about it: Orthodox worship seems to be the height of formality, the epitome of fossilized ritual. Why, the major elements of the Sunday morning service have not significantly changed in over sixteen hundred years! Now, for the average Protestant, that fact alone would be enough to condemn Orthodox liturgy. How can that kind of worship represent anything but empty, anachronistic, legalistic religion? It's certainly not what I was looking for.

As someone who all my adult life was intimately involved in leading the worship experience, I know something about modern Protestant worship. What the Protestant is looking for, and what pastors and worship leaders are hoping to provide, is a worship experience that is "meaningful." What does "meaningful" mean? First, the music needs to inspire people to feel love and devotion for God, and allow them the opportunity to express those feelings. Secondly, the sermon needs to give them something fresh and meaty to ponder—something that will inspire the congregation to follow God.

If I'm sitting in the pews, my goal is "to get something out of this"—to find godly joy and inspiration. What do I need in order for that to happen? Just what the leaders are trying to give me—good music and a good sermon.

So what happens if the music isn't that great, or isn't the style that I prefer? What if the preacher isn't very dynamic, or constantly speaks over or under my head? Well, then the worship experience won't be what I'd hoped for. If this problem persists from week to week, I may find it easy to stay home, or go to the beach and commune with God in that great "cathedral of the outdoors." Or, if I'm a more committed Christian, I'll eventually decide it's time to go somewhere else and see if a different church can give me the worship music and the solid sermons I need in order to grow in the Lord.

Worship and Obedience

Having lived in both worlds, I can tell you the critical difference between Protestant worship and Orthodox worship. Simply put, Protestants come to church primarily to learn something about God; Orthodox faithful, on the other hand, come to worship God. Now, don't get me wrong: what a Protestant wants to get from worship is something of a spiritual nature. He comes to receive godly inspiration from the music and the teaching.

But something different motivates the Orthodox worshiper. He comes to church mainly out of simple obedience to the Holy God who calls for our adoration. The point that needs to be grasped by the Protestant who wants to understand liturgical worship is this: When the primary goal of a worshiper is to gain inspiration, ritual worship may seem pointless. But when his objective is to give obedient reverence, ritual worship is the only type of worship that makes any sense.

After all, it's obvious that you can't be perfectly obedient to someone unless that person gives you clear, straightforward directions to obey. This is especially true in the case of erring human creatures who are seeking to obey God. For our sakes, the Lord must be specific about what He wants. What's more, because of our sinful ignorance, He cannot constantly change His directions.

With this in mind, let me contrast the Protestant and Orthodox experiences more carefully. A Protestant attends church in the hope that something will happen, at least on most Sundays, to stir him. Excellent music might be enough to accomplish that. But what the Protestant worshiper really needs is for the pastor to give him something to think about that he's never thought about before— something that will make God come alive in his soul. From a rationalist point of view, it's obvious that a person can't stay inspired unless he hears something new, or hears something he's heard before in a fresh, more stimulating way.

Once again, the Protestant religious experience starts in the mind.

That being the case, ritual worship is not going to help. How is worship that's essentially the same every time going to stimulate me with new things to think about? I've got to receive fresh, inspiring input in order to live for God and to grow spiritually. So liturgical worship is out. I need something more moving, more "meaningful."

Thus, at the end of each Sunday service, Protestant ministers and lay people always have a judgment call to make: How "meaningful" was the service? Were the minister and worship team "in tune" with God, making it a great day? Was it just spiritually mediocre? Or does the church board really need to make some changes in personnel? Some weeks the answers are positive; sometimes they're not. But any honest Protestant will tell you that worship does not pass muster until these judgments have been made.

When I was a Protestant minister, a woman I knew worked as the hostess in a popular after-church restaurant. One day she told me that any time I wanted to know how good a job my fellow pastors around town were doing, I could just ask her. "Sometimes they're on pedestals," she observed, "but most of the time, they're on crosses."

Of course, in evaluating the pastor over lunch, Protestant believers are demonstrating how much is riding on their need for inspiration. If the pastor and the choir aren't providing it, they feel that their spiritual lives are stagnating. They worry about that.

Now, can you imagine attending a church where the power and effectiveness of the worship experience do not depend primarily upon the creative excellence of the pastor or the choir? Where the worship can be fulfilling every time? This is Orthodox worship. Why is it that way? It's precisely because it is *liturgical*, and because its primary motivation is the right worship of God the Father, the Son, and the Holy Spirit.

Sunday Morning Comin' Down

Let me briefly describe for you my typical Sunday morning experience as an Orthodox Christian. First of all, we skip breakfast—even the coffee! The Church has always fasted before the Eucharist in anticipation of receiving, as the first food of the day, the Body and Blood of Christ. As I leave for church, there is one thought, one objective, in my mind: "Today, I will give praise and honor to Christ. For He calls me to come meet with Him, to be united with Him." There is no anxiety, not even the hint of a question, about whether it will be meaningful. It will, because nothing can hinder it. (Of course, it's true that my *perception* of its meaning can be hindered if I am inattentive or if I come to worship with a heart that has not been cleansed of sin. But that fault is in me, not in the Liturgy or in those who celebrate it.)

Why do I have that confidence? Strange as it may sound, it's because the Holy Spirit will make this occur through the service itself—not primarily through those who perform it. The Church's liturgical worship, you see, is not the invention of men. It is a gift that the Church received in its infancy from the Spirit who would lead her into all truth. The liturgical services of the Church are the embodiment of Christ's directions to His Apostles as to how we must worship Him.

Now, again, I know my Protestant reader is not just going to accept that assertion immediately. He can certainly discover its truth if he likes, just as I did. But what I ask the reader to do at this point is at least to grant this: If the Liturgy is God-given, then all the beautiful things I'm going to say about it in these next pages would have to be absolutely true. I would also ask my Protestant reader to entertain this thought: Doesn't the worship I'm describing here really sound like the way worship ought to be?

The Orthodox Christian worships in an environment where God Himself directs the acts of worship; the Protestant, on the other hand, must hope that God can somehow inspire people to create meaningful acts of worship. Can you grasp the great difference? When God defines the acts, sinful, erring people can't get in the way of their success. And when the acts He requires to be performed are always the same, His worshipers can never be confused, or be led into false worship by the ever-subtle enemy.

When worship is like this, wonderful things happen. Think about it. Every prayer the worshipers raise must be answered, because God Himself has declared what shall be petitioned. Every song will be to His glory, for He has ordained the words. Every act will be in submission to His Spirit, for He has declared what shall be done. So, when an Orthodox Christian faithfully and willingly does what God asks, his worship is full of God.

But there is a paradox here. When an Orthodox Christian comes to liturgical worship obediently and participates wholeheartedly, he also ends up getting the *inspiration* for which the Protestant so sincerely longs. So as an Orthodox believer, the thought, "Will the service be good today?" never enters my mind. The question, "Will I be inspired by church today?" never enters my mind. The service is always good, the worship is right, and whether I get inspired or not is entirely up to me.

Now, I'm not saying that there aren't some days when the choir sings better than others. Some priests have much better voices for chanting the Liturgy than others, and some are better preachers. Certainly beautiful singing and clear preaching make for a more aesthetically pleasing Liturgy than poor singing and preaching.

But the beauty and power of the Spirit-inspired Liturgy is this: feeble and undependable human agents cannot stand between God's people and an experience of the fullness of God's blessings. For the intimacy of our moments with God is not riding on the thrilling quality of the music or on the originality of the sermon. The power of the Liturgy is not found in the talents of the priest and the singers. No, the power of the Liturgy is found within the sacramental acts performed in it. All the priest and singers must do is present the Liturgy, opening the way for us to come to the Sacrament with faith and obedient adoration.

This is why liturgical worship is the only kind of worship God has *ever* ordained! The chosen people of Israel worshiped liturgically. (We learned that in our evangelical Bible training.) Nowhere in the Old Testament did they ever "wing it" in the temple! Therefore, liturgical worship was also the only kind of worship the Apostles knew. My old belief that the worship of the early Church was similar to that of a home fellowship group was really nonsensical. The Apostles could not have conceived of such worship. Nor did the

Holy Spirit teach it to them. He altered only the object of their worship. Christ—especially through the celebration of His Eucharist—becomes the Centerpiece of Christian liturgy.

Let me return to my Sunday morning routine. When I enter the church, I step into heaven. Literally. Mystically, yes, but nevertheless literally. The sanctuary of an Orthodox church is patterned on the descriptions of heaven found in the Books of Isaiah and Revelation. There is the altar, the Throne of God. With it are the lampstands and the incense that those scriptural passages describe. Surrounding the throne are angels and saints, whom I see through the "windows" of their icons. Every time I walk through the door of the sanctuary, I am swept into the holy river of worship that is always flowing there. Just by entering that sanctuary, I am humbled. My heart and my eyes are opened, and I begin to see that I have indeed come to

> Mount Zion and to the city of the living God, the heavenly Jerusalem, to an innumerable company of angels, to the general assembly and church of the firstborn who are registered in heaven, to God the Judge of all, to the spirits of just men made perfect, to Jesus the Mediator of the new covenant, and to the blood of sprinkling that speaks better things than that of Abel (Hebrews 12:22–24).

In the midst of this glorious scene I stand, ready obediently to worship my Creator and God. Then the priest cries, "Blessed is the Kingdom of the Father, and of the Son, and of the Holy Spirit, now and ever, and unto the ages of ages." The whole congregation sings the "Amen."

Thus begins a sublime worship, which is almost entirely chanted and sung. The priest and congregation sing beautiful prayers, the priest making supplication, the congregation responding after each line with "Lord, have mercy" or "Grant this, O Lord." Hymns of praise as old as the Church itself are lifted in holy joy. With ceremonious honor and reverence, the Epistle and Gospel are read. Then there is a pause in the singing, as the priest gives a homily (sermon) on the Gospel reading. (In some churches, the homily is given at the end of the Liturgy.) Usually, the emphasis of the priest is on teaching the people how to live according to the words they have just heard. This first part of the service is called the liturgy of the Word.

When the homily is finished, the prayers and hymns begin anew. We now move into the Eucharistic liturgy. The focus shifts to the miraculous and holy event that is about to occur. In the songs and prayers, we hear deep humility, repentance, and trembling gratitude, as Christ comes as both the Offerer and the Offering of the Eucharist. We profess the Nicene Creed, as Christians have done for over sixteen hundred years. We pray that Christ will forgive us and mercifully allow us unworthy ones to receive His transforming Body and Blood. Then, stepping forth from the altar bearing the Eucharist, the priest exclaims, "In the fear of God, and with faith and love, draw near." The faithful go forward and receive from the same chalice the Holy Gifts of Christ's Presence.

Afterward, the hymns swell with awesome thanksgiving and praise. Under a multitude of blessings, those empowered by the enlivening Spirit go forth to live lives of chastity, prayer, fasting, and holiness—lives of oneness with the Redeemer who has given them His Life.

When faithful Orthodox Christians meet for coffee or lunch after the service, they really have nothing to complain about! Because their worship is liturgical and not innovative, there's nothing that the priest or the choir (be its singing beautiful or not-so-beautiful) could have done to prevent them from meeting God. They know they have received the blessing of Christ's enlivening Body and Blood in the Eucharist. All that intimate union and communion with God can be, they have touched and tasted in worship.

Growth and Change

What a world of difference there is between this and modern Protestant services. Still, my Protestant reader may be concerned that no matter how glorious and moving the Divine Liturgy may be, worship that is the same from week to week cannot possibly foster growth in God. After all, doesn't growth require change? That seems to be a law everywhere, in the natural world and in the spiritual. Sameness in worship would seem to inspire stagnation, not development.

Absolutely, growth requires change. Spiritual growth especially demands it, because there is so much in us sinful creatures that needs alteration. The big question is, "How does spiritual refinement occur in an individual, and what kind of worship will best promote that process?"

I think an Orthodox Christian and a Protestant would agree that the goal of spiritual growth must be to become like Christ. How, though, does one determine what kind of worship encourages that spiritual evolution? It seems clear that for one's worship to make him like Jesus, the believer's worship must reflect Christ our God—who He is, what He does. He is Love. He is the Redeemer. He is the Creator. He orders all things. All creation serves and honors Him. He is also *changeless*. In Him, St. James says, "is no variation or shadow of turning" (James 1:17). The writer of Hebrews (according to Orthodox Tradition, St. Paul) reminds us that "Jesus Christ is the same yesterday, today, and forever" (Hebrews 13:8).

It is evident that these characteristics are reflected dynamically in the Divine Liturgy. Love stands as its centerpiece in the form of the Holy Eucharist—the celebration of the awesome and merciful sacrifice of Christ. Every act within the Liturgy has been created and ordered by the Spirit of God, not by His creatures. By its nature, the Liturgy requires everyone present, priest and layman alike, to actively and humbly participate in honoring the Triune God. In its eminent constancy (no essential alterations in sixteen centuries), it serves as an incredible example of God's invariable nature. The Liturgy bears brightly the express Image of the Godhead.

But what about contemporary Protestant worship? Whereas in the Orthodox Church the focal point is the altar, at the center of the Protestant service is the pulpit. The main thrust is preaching and teaching—good things to be sure, but not worship. The details of the service are as changeable as the desires and tastes of those who create them, and bear little resemblance to historic biblical worship.

Very little participation is required from the congregation, who might just as well be referred to as the "audience." In fact, the place of assembly is often called the "auditorium," the "listening post." The service's success or failure is judged by how well those who officiate perform in pleasing the congregation.

I finally came to realize that when I was a Protestant, I judged the quality of worship by what it did for *me,* not what it did to exalt *God.* The question, "Did I offer to God every obedience that He asked of me today?" almost never entered my mind. Having no specific understanding of how God's people had always worshiped, I could not have answered it anyway. Rather, I gauged the effectiveness of my worship experience by how inspiring it was for me. Given my rationalism—which is driven by the desire for new information—I couldn't measure it any other way.

Liturgical worship is like a refining fire. It never goes out. God shines forth in it, in all His glory. When I come to it, I must yield to the God who is revealed in it. I speak the words He commands. I sing the songs He calls forth. I pray the prayers He enjoins me to pray. What He desires, I must adhere to. What He wants done, I must do. There is no room for concern over myself or my wants. What is this worship, other than an opportunity for me to become like Christ?

✦ 15 ✦

Formal Prayer

The power of liturgical worship to break the willful spirit, and to inspire the heart with submissive and grateful adoration, carries over into the Orthodox believer's personal prayer life. For Orthodox believers, even private prayer is sacramental. As he looks at Orthodox prayer, however, the typical Protestant will likely shudder. He will see me reciting prayers from my prayer book, shake his head, and say, "How can you pray so mindlessly? How can you ever have a real and honest relationship with God unless you express yourself to Him?" I know that until a few years ago, that's what I would have said. (Of course, in saying such things my Protestant friends and I were forgetting that we had been singing written and memorized hymns all our lives, and never saw any problem whatsoever with that!)

This response manifests the basic picture of prayer that guides a modern Protestant in his attempts to commune with God. For prayer to be meaningful to him, it must be a sort of casual conversation between himself and God. That's the way I prayed all my life. So it was rather amazing to discover that this is not at all the ancient Church's understanding of true prayer.

Screwtape on Spontaneity

How did I miss, when I first read it years ago, what C. S. Lewis has to say about the spontaneous, self-expressing prayer that I typically offered as an evangelical? In Lewis' *The Screwtape Letters*, the Archdemon Screwtape corresponds with his nephew demon, Wormwood. Screwtape is giving his young apprentice advice as to how to prevent his assigned human "patient" from becoming a true Christian. With regard to prayer, Screwtape says:

The best thing, where it is possible, is to keep the patient from the serious intention of praying altogether. When the patient is an adult recently reconverted to the Enemy's party [by "Enemy," of course, the demon means God], like your man, this is best done by encouraging him to remember, or to think he remembers, the parrot-like nature of prayers in childhood. In reaction against that, *he may be persuaded to aim at something entirely spontaneous, inward, informal, and unregularised* . . . in which real concentration of will and intelligence have no part. . . . *That is exactly the sort of prayer we want*; and since it bears a superficial resemblance to the prayer of silence as practiced by those who are very far advanced in the Enemy's service, *clever and lazy patients can be taken in by it for quite a long time* (italics mine).[1]

I don't know what I thought when I read that as a Protestant. But C. S. Lewis obviously knew that the only kind of prayer that reliably defeats the demons is either the prayer of silence (which only the most spiritually advanced are able to practice effectively), or prayer that is formal, planned, regular, and focused away from my inward feelings. You know what? That's Orthodox prayer!

To pray this way, I obviously cannot improvise prayers off-the-cuff. Instead, I offer prayers that the Church provides for me— prayers that have been proven in the Church to produce deep repentance, humility, profound gratitude, and an intimate sense of union with God. When practiced in this formal way, my prayer becomes something more profound and holy than a spontaneous, casual conversation with God. It becomes a sacramental act of obedient and selfless interaction with God.

Now a Protestant may find it difficult to understand how praying prayers that are not "personal" can lead to a deeply personal communion with God. It seems paradoxical. I've learned, however, that paradox is God's trademark! It's to be expected from a God who assures us, "My thoughts are not your thoughts" (Isaiah 55:8).

But it's important for a Protestant to understand why C. S. Lewis alarmingly (and correctly) observes that the demons are pleased when we pray "spontaneous, inward, informal, and unregularised" prayers. To see the problem, we first need to consider what the ultimate purpose of prayer is. Then, we must recognize why spontaneous prayers, by their very nature, cannot truly fulfill that purpose. Finally, we must see how praying in the formal Orthodox fashion unlocks the heart's door to allow it to experience the regenerating Presence of God.

The Purpose of Prayer

St. Paul teaches us that by "beholding" the "glory of the Lord," we are "transformed" into the very "image" of our Savior (2 Corinthians 3:18). How do we behold the glory of the Lord? We behold Him within the deep heart of true prayer. As St. Silouan the Athonite tells us, prayer is the means by which the soul may

> dwell in the love of God, for the grace of the Holy Spirit comes through prayer. Prayer preserves a man from sin, for the prayerful mind stays intent on God, *and in humbleness of spirit stands before the Face of the Lord*, Whom the soul of him who prays knoweth (italics mine).[2]

Reflected in the words of these servants of Christ is a clear understanding that prayer is much more than the act of presenting God with a list of the things I need from Him. It even transcends the offering of praise, or the expression to Him of my gratitude and thanksgiving. Ultimately prayer is a sacramental act in which I meet God face-to-face. In that place, I can really hear Him. He can truly speak to me. Through such encounters, I may be changed into His likeness, according to His will.

Ultimately, then, prayer serves as the instrument of my transformation. The problem with spontaneous, conversational, self-expressing prayer is that it can actually thwart the whole process of regeneration. Why? Because spontaneous prayer suffers from the old rationalism problem. Praying that way, I'm stuck in the world of ideas, words, and images. I am kept from encountering Jesus as the Person He is.

How Do You Hear God?

It seems to me that there are at least three ways in which the spontaneous, "talk with Jesus as with a friend" model of prayer—pretty much the standard among evangelical Protestants—gets in the way of really experiencing the life-changing Presence of God.

First of all, this type of prayer is so "noisy" that it keeps the one who prays from actually hearing God. Let me explain what I mean. I think most believers would agree that the ability to hear God speak to our souls is certainly crucial in the process of transformation. But we know, just as Elijah discovered, that the Almighty typically speaks to us in a "still small voice" (1 Kings 19:12). What must I do to hear that still small voice when I pray? I must be very, very quiet. "Be still, and know that I am God," writes the psalmist (Psalm 46:10).

That is why, as C. S. Lewis rightly notes, the most advanced in the spiritual realm pray in complete silence. Now, that doesn't mean they say words of prayer under their breath or in their minds. It means that they pray deep within the heart, in the mysterious place the ancient Church calls the *nous*. That's where the Holy Spirit dwells. In the *nous*, all human words, feelings, and thoughts are left behind. There is only the Spirit, enveloping those who abide there in the holy silence of uncreated Light.

But spontaneous prayer cannot lead me to that most quiet place. Why? First of all, praying spontaneously requires me to construct my prayer. I must decide what I'm going to pray about and how I'm going to express those things to God. I must follow my thoughts as they flow through my mind. All that mental "noise" makes hearing God's still small voice in the absolute quiet of the *nous* a virtual impossibility.

More Than Just a Friend

Secondly, there's a problem with the "talk to Jesus like a friend" aspect of modern spontaneous prayer. Now, I can attest from personal experience that the contemporary emphasis on conversational prayer merely reflects the deep yearning many Protestants have to be close to God. By His grace, their hearts are aware of Him, and they long to touch Him, to commune with Him—to know Him as an intimate friend.

Without question, we should experience Jesus' friendship; He is, after all, a "friend who sticks closer than a brother" (Proverbs 18:24). But what about those times when the Lord might want to relate to the praying believer as something other than a friend? The mature one who prays in silence knows that sometimes Jesus comes as the Creator whose overwhelming Presence leaves him prostrate, or as the Lifegiver whose unrelenting goodness makes him sob with gratitude, or as the holy and terrible Judge before whom his soul—and body!—literally quake in heartbroken repentance, or as the Almighty King whose gaze he keenly senses could consume him in a flash.

Moment by moment, the Lord presents Himself to us as He desires. To know Christ as He is requires more than just trying to think about Him as a friend. To truly experience Him requires a way of prayer that is able to recognize whatever face He chooses to reveal to us in a given moment.

Simply put, my spontaneous, conversational prayer doesn't allow me to respond to Jesus that way. It can't keep up with Christ, so to speak. Thus, the best it can achieve is a rather one-sided conversation with a predetermined image of Christ that I have fixed in my mind. Recognizing the serious limitations of this kind of communing with God, is it any wonder that the most common complaint I heard as a Protestant minister was, "Pastor, why is it that my prayers never seem to get any higher than the ceiling?"

Passionate Prayer

The third flaw in spontaneous prayer is also a serious one. You see, when my method of prayer is just to open my heart and express myself, my prayers often end up being just exactly that—expressions of *self.* Instead of being focused on God, I'm focused on myself—and there's no way I can escape the spotlight. After all, my prayers are my own words. In them, I declare *my* views, *my* feelings, *my* wants, *my* needs, and *my* desires.

But what's wrong with that, so long as I'm honestly expressing to God what's in my heart? Well, what is in my heart, anyway? The Prophet Jeremiah disconcertingly informs me that my heart is "deceitful above all things, / And desperately wicked" (Jeremiah 17:9). Every selfish desire of the flesh dwells there.

On the other hand, St. Paul tells me that because I am a believer in Christ, "God has sent forth the Spirit of His Son" into my heart (Galatians 4:6). So my heart turns out to be the seat of both godly desires and selfish ones. Thus, it seems that I face a dilemma when I just spontaneously pour forth prayer from my heart: do the words coming out of my mouth express Spirit-filled sentiments, or self-centered, ungodly ones?

Since the heart is deceitful, telling the difference is not easy. Most believers, I think, will agree that the heart is adept at making selfish desires seem like godly ones. I think of the many times I've asked God to help me accomplish something for His glory, completely blind to the fact that it was my own selfish ego I was really looking to satisfy. Other times, I've implored the Lord to change a brother's heart toward me, without realizing that I was just trying to avoid changing my stubborn and self-righteous attitude toward him.

There is a kind of prayer that can reveal to me the hidden selfishness behind my godly words and bring me to healing repentance, all within the very act of praying. That kind of prayer is powerful and transforming. Unfortunately, the kind of spontaneous, conversational prayer I grew up praying cannot produce that kind of experience.

Why? Consider this. For my prayer to reveal the concealed sinfulness within me, it must somehow allow God to show me what is really in my heart. When the way I pray lets me see myself through God's eyes, my hidden passions will be illumined like fugitives cowering in a searchlight's blinding beam.

On the other hand, spontaneous prayer is just the process of me telling God what is in my heart. That kind of prayer can never show me God's view of what is wise or what is right. And it certainly can never reveal and transform the veiled iniquity in my soul. To expect it to do so is a little like hoping the fleeing fugitive will turn the searchlight upon himself.

Praying Sacramentally

We can see, then, why Screwtape would say that the demons love it when we pray spontaneously. As long as we're doing that, we are keeping ourselves from experiencing the transforming power of God. We make their job easier.

Even when I was a Protestant who prayed conversationally, I recognized some of these issues. I knew I couldn't hear God speak to me when I wasn't letting Him get a word in edgewise. So the picture I developed of how prayer works is that you take turns—you talk to Him, then try to be quiet and let Him talk to you.

But even that picture of prayer is different from what the ancient Church has always taught and practiced. The Church understands prayer, like any other sacrament, as an act of worship in which we stand before God "with unveiled face," "beholding" the "glory of the Lord," thereby being "transformed" into His "image" (2 Corinthians 3:18).

I can tell you from experience, when one begins to practice this kind of prayer, he finds himself in a different world. He gets the overwhelming sense that for the first time in his life, he's experiencing prayer as it's really meant to be experienced.

And who would ever guess that this beautiful encounter with God all starts with a prayer book?

The Rite of Prayer

What's in a prayer book, anyway? If you look in my Orthodox prayer book, you'll find many of the Psalms, as well as the prayers of men whose lives the Church recognizes as exceptionally holy. These prayers are there because they have proven themselves effective in opening the hearts of those who offer them to the transforming Presence of God.

You'll also see that the prayers are divided into various sections: Morning Prayers, Evening Prayers, canons (special prayer-songs offered for specific purposes), akathists (which one might describe as love poems to God and His saints), along with prayers for numerous special situations and needs.

So how does offering the prayers from this book bring me to a life-altering encounter with Christ? Well, this kind of praying does all the important things that spontaneous prayer does not. It quiets the mind so that I can hear God in my heart. It allows me to see myself through God's eyes, and to know His healing touch. In short, formal prayer leads me to an encounter with God as He is.

Renewing the Mind

St. Paul admonishes Christians to "be transformed by the renewing of your mind" (Romans 12:2). Prayers that fill my mind with the sound of my own voice and express my own thoughts and feelings do not contribute much to the renewal process. I need to hear God's voice, God's words.

As I said earlier, when it comes to hearing God, nothing beats a completely silent mind. But that is not a state that one achieves overnight. You see, the mind is by nature active. Even when I was a Protestant, I used to try to quiet my mind in order to listen to God. But before I knew it, I'd find I was thinking about the test I had to grade, or the oil change my car needed, or a million other thoughts on which my mind would light as it flitted about.

When I pray in the Orthodox way, I can still encounter the same problem. But I've discovered that I can at least begin to control my praying mind. By the grace of God, I can learn to bring my prayers, like all my other thoughts, "into captivity to the obedience of Christ" (2 Corinthians 10:5). How? Simply by praying words that are not my own.

It is amazing what happens when I start to pray the petitions of holy men from my prayer book. Even though my mind may not be perfectly quiet, at least the "me" within my prayers is silenced. The prayers I used to work so hard to create, and which often deceptively gave voice to my self-centeredness, are now replaced by words that are perfect in their humility, selflessness, love, and gratitude.

Oh, I still struggle with distracting thoughts. But now, it's much easier to bring my mind back to focus on the prayers. They're right there, in black and white. When I prayed spontaneously, the only way I could escape "unprayerful" distractions was to create different, "prayerful" thoughts. I realize now that in doing that, I was just forcing my mind to come up with distractions for my distractions. That certainly did nothing to quiet my mind and make it more attentive to God.

Growing in the Experience of God

In reciting prayers from a prayer book, I take the first important steps toward encountering God "as He is" in the depths of my heart. Offering these prayers, I assure that what is in my mind is completely consistent with anything God might whisper in my heart. Or put another way, I could say that I know the words of my prayers tell the truth about God, and about me. By learning how to come back to the words of those prayers when I am distracted, I am learning how to let go of my own self-created thoughts, and focus my attention on holy words that come from another Source. All this turning away from myself—from my own thoughts, words, and imaginings—humbles me, and opens my heart to the transforming power of God.

Every Orthodox saint who's ever written on prayer sees the next step in a believer's growth as one in which prayer descends from the mind into the heart. Perhaps more correctly, they would say that the mind itself descends into the heart.[3]

That's a strange saying. What does it mean, exactly? It means that in the journey toward the pure prayer of silence, God brings the believer to a place where the mind leaves behind its distractions. It becomes entirely focused on the words of the prayer. When I say "focused on the words," I'm not saying that the mind starts to analyze the *meanings* of the words. No, that would be distracting. Instead, the holiness in the prayer's words becomes a sort of bridge between the mind and heart. By focusing on them, the mind leaves behind the concerns of earthly life and crosses fully and attentively into the *nous,* into the Presence of the indwelling Spirit. Through such an act of prayer, the fulfillment of the commandment to "love the LORD your God with all your heart, with all your soul, with all your mind, and with all your strength" (Mark 12:30) becomes a real possibility.

In that place, we begin to see Christ as He is, as He reveals Himself in the moment. We let go of our preconceived images of Him. What's more, in the light of His reality, we come face-to-face with our own sinfulness. No longer can it cleverly hide itself behind the self-generated words of our prayers.

The holy ones who pray in silence are those who, by the grace of God, have transcended even the need for the bridge of words. These blessed ones simply dwell in the *nous*, beholding like the Apostles on the Mount of Transfiguration the glorious Light of God (see Matthew 17). Since I've become Orthodox, I've had the very humbling privilege of meeting some of those mystically sweet and eminently quiet souls who by the grace of Christ have entered that place. Their eyes seem as deep as the universe.

Praying in the Moment
Still, someone might ask, "Is there *never* a time for spontaneous, informal prayer? What about prayers of intercession for others? What about those emergency situations when prayer must be raised in the moment—and I don't have time to grab a prayer book? Or what of those occasions when repentance and gratitude toward God literally overwhelm the heart?"

The fact is, the ancient Church even gives us prayers that allow us to meet the specific needs of the moment. For instance, in the case of intercession, a helpful approach is to drop names and specific needs into the appropriate places in a litany—a formal prayer of supplication. This way, we can pray very specifically and yet utilize the unifying prayers of the Church in the process. Of course, one can also pray in one's own words; it's not forbidden. But over time, the words of liturgical prayer begin to come more naturally to the lips than the old, "I just really want to ask you, Lord . . ."

Finally, let me say a word about the centuries-old "Jesus Prayer." It's incredibly simple and is used by Christians the world over—often in times of emergency, or when one is not sure how to pray, or when all other words fail. It goes like this:

Lord Jesus Christ, Son of God, have mercy on me, a sinner.

This short prayer is a wonderful confession of Jesus Christ as Lord and God, and a personal declaration of repentance and love. It can be offered for oneself or for others. Through this prayer one invokes the mercy of Christ, and displays a simple trust in His infinite wisdom and goodness. That quiet, selfless trust is the foundation of all true prayer.

→ 16 ←

Mary, the Theotokos

Along with the acts of true worship that he offers to God, a pious Orthodox Christian also offers heartfelt veneration to Mary the Mother of God and to the saints. The Church recognizes these holy people as being exemplary in their Christlikeness. Note carefully that our worship is directed toward God. We do not worship Mary or the saints. Veneration is not worship, but rather an expression of love, honor, and respect for those who by their lives, and by their deaths, have defended and kept the precious Faith alive for us. They have paved the way to heaven for us with their holy prayers, their works, their tears, and even their blood.

Typically in the Church this veneration is expressed by kissing the icons of the Theotokos (Greek for "Mother of God," the term by which Orthodox generally refer to Mary) and of the saints. In doing this, the Orthodox Christian is not being idolatrous. He is not worshiping a picture. Instead, he is giving his love to the one who is depicted in the icon.

Nor is the icon just a picture. It is rather a prayerful, divinely inspired, artistic capturing of the Spirit of Christ as it is revealed in the life of the blessed saint. Truly, as some Orthodox hymns honoring saints explicitly declare, veneration is the act of "praising Christ *in* His saints."

This is another aspect of the Orthodox Christian life that initially made me recoil. And I know I'm not alone! So how did I come to change my mind? Let me explain.

In a corner of my living room stands a large bookcase. Along with books and knick-knacks, we keep family pictures on it. One of the photographs there is of my beloved younger brother, Barry. He was killed in an auto accident in 1976, at the age of twenty-one.

Simply to say that I loved my brother does not adequately capture my feelings for him. A quarter of a century has passed since his death; yet I still awaken each twenty-seventh day of July (his birthday) with a tear in my eye, and with the bittersweet pain of remembrance glowing in my heart.

Now, not one of my Protestant friends would think it strange if, while standing before that bookshelf, I were to pick up Barry's photograph and give it a kiss. But what happens when I take two large strides to the right to my icon shelf, and kiss the icon of Mary, the Theotokos? Now, suddenly, I'm an idolater. What changed? What's wrong with Mary, that she's not worthy of the kind of love and respect I would give to my departed brother?

Or suppose I kiss the icon of my daughter's patron saint, Vera. Just like my brother Barry, she died a violent death. Nineteen centuries ago, at the age of twelve, she was martyred for the sake of Christ, along with her mother and two younger sisters. But in Protestant eyes, showing her the kind of love I would give to my brother is a sinful thing to do.

Just what is the problem here? When I began to struggle with this issue, I saw something paradoxical in my old Protestant attitudes. On the one hand, I would condemn people who honored Mary and the saints; yet on the other hand, I saw nothing wrong with honoring respected Protestant preachers and teachers, living or dead. It was perfectly okay to sing the praises of these people, to watch videos and slide shows that recounted their deeds, and get all misty-eyed as someone performed "Thank You for Giving to the Lord." But if I saw someone giving laud and honor to the woman who bore the Savior in her womb—why, the very act made that person's Christianity questionable!

There Is Something Special about Mary

When I discuss this issue of veneration with some of my Protestant friends, they become vehement, almost caustic—especially when we speak of the Theotokos. The reason they give for their disdain of this practice is almost always expressed in the same way. I heard it in a conversation just the other day, as an old friend angrily cried, almost spitting the words, "There's nothing special about Mary! She's no different from anyone else!"

When I hear that kind of reaction, I know that there is more involved here than in the average doctrinal dispute. This is an issue that many of my Protestant friends seem to take personally. But having been in their shoes, it is not hard for me to understand their impassioned resistance. It has its root in "it's just Jesus and me" theology, in that radical individualism which forms the foundation of the typical Protestant's faith.

I'll carefully consider that last point in the next chapter. For now, I'd like to address the question, "Is there nothing special about Mary?" Typically, when I try to talk about these things with my Protestant friends, I first must listen to them tell me what I believe about the Theotokos. So to begin with, let me deal with some of the points they raise.

Who Is Mary?

Usually, my Protestant friends insist that I believe Mary is somehow equal to God, and that I worship her as divine. Nothing could be further from the truth. Mary was born with the same corrupt human nature as you and I. (The "immaculate conception" is a Roman Catholic doctrine, not an Orthodox one.) She tasted death, just like all who bear the curse of fallenness. She is not God, and thus cannot be worshiped.

My friends tell me that I believe I can't pray directly to Christ—that all my prayers have to go through Mary, or through one of the saints. It is true that I address the Theotokos and the saints in my prayers—although to say I pray "to" them is not accurate. Actually, I simply ask them to do what I frequently ask my earthly Christian brothers and sisters to do: offer intercessory prayer for me.

And the truth is, such supplications represent only a small portion of my prayer life. For instance, if you look at my prayer book, you will see that the morning prayers take up about thirty pages. Those that invoke Mary and the saints take up roughly three of those pages. The rest are offered to the Trinity—to the Father, Son, and Holy Spirit, either collectively or individually. All Orthodox

Christians rejoice in the truth that with His death, Christ purchased for each of us direct access to the Godhead. So the accusations of my friends in this regard are without any foundation.

If for nothing else, my friends will chastise me for giving Mary the title I give her—the Theotokos, the Mother of God. They insist that she should not be given such an exalted name. But they would not dispute that she gave birth to Christ. What, then, should we call her?

When I worked through this question, I was again forced to confront my Protestant rationalism. A Protestant's chief concern, you see, is with the things Jesus did. As a Protestant, my theological focus was almost entirely upon the work of Christ, in His ministry and on the Cross. What was important to me were the spiritual concepts He taught and the salvation He accomplished. Rarely did I ever find myself thinking about the fact that He even had a mother. Who she was seemed entirely immaterial. Certainly there was no need to think of her as the Mother of God. To me, she was just Mary. In the shadow of those things I considered most important in the plan of salvation, it was easy to forget she has any real relationship to the Child she carried in her womb.

But when you face the fact that Mary *is* Jesus' mother, you realize that what you call her must be entirely consistent with who you believe Jesus to be. That is, you don't want to call Mary something that would give the wrong impression about her Son. In considering this problem, the bishops at the Council of Ephesus, which in 431 officially gave Mary the title *Theotokos* (though Christian writings going back to the second century refer to her by that name), reasoned this way:

If the one in Mary's womb was simply a man, she should be called *Anthropotokos*—"mother of a man." If the one within her womb was just a man on whom God bestowed a special spirit—the "Christ-spirit"—then Mary should be known as "mother of the Christ," or *Christotokos*.

But the Church believes that He who resided within the womb of Mary was one of the Holy Trinity, God the Son, equal in nature to the Father. In her womb, the Son of God took on full human nature, while never ceasing to be God. In her womb, He possessed the same two natures that He possesses now as Ruler of the universe—He was fully God and fully man. Thus, to call Mary anything less than *Theotokos*—the Mother of God—actually amounts to a *denial* of who Jesus Christ is. Calling her anything less denies the truth of the Incarnation, that Jesus Christ is at once God and man.

"Blessed Art Thou Among Women"

Once I get past these questions with my friends, I can begin to relate the obvious characteristics that show the Theotokos to be unique—the most blessed and most important human being who has ever been created. First of all, Mary is the only person in the universe who has ever given to God something God did not already possess—human nature. For the humanity her divine Son now possesses, He gained from her.

Here is an obvious point that I don't remember ever considering when I was a Protestant. When God decides to become Incarnate for the salvation of man, He faces a problem. In the Garden of Eden, mankind had freely rejected Him. Now, God respects the free will of His human creatures. Thus, He cannot simply say, "I will become human and save mankind, whether they want Me to or not." God will not force Himself upon us that way. The curse of God's absence had fallen upon all humanity as a result of Eve's rejecting Him. For the curse to be removed, someone—not surprisingly, another woman—must lovingly, selflessly, and obediently embrace Him, receiving Him back on behalf of all humanity.

And so, we hear these incredibly important words spoken by Mary, after Gabriel had proclaimed to her God's intentions: "Behold the maidservant of the Lord! Let it be to me according to your word" (Luke 1:38). Here we come face to face with a truth that should make every one of us shed tears of gratitude before this Blessed Virgin: If Mary does not say "Yes," there is no Incarnation. And if there is no Incarnation, there is no salvation for mankind.

Immediately, my Protestant friends reply, "Well, God would have just found someone else." In fact, Orthodox Tradition tells us that God had been preparing for this particular virgin to fill this role for generations. He provided a godly family for her to be born into so that she would be as pure as a fallen human can be—pure enough to receive the Son of God. If she had refused, the process of preparation would have had to begin all over again, and another virgin would be the one Orthodox Christians revere. But *some* young woman had to freely, of her own will, open the door to God for all of us, just as Eve had closed it. *And it was precious Mary.* Thus, as Eve was mother of the fallen race, so Mary is mother of the redeemed.

What a debt we owe her! She has had an active role in the salvation of every human being who has ever come to Christ. For she has born the One who saves each one of us. How then, can my friend so mindlessly exclaim, "There's nothing special about Mary!"?

When I hear my Protestant friends speak with such disdain of the Theotokos, I am pained for their sakes, and I wonder if they have ever considered this: They are speaking disparagingly about the mother of the One who wrote with His finger on tablets of stone, "Honor thy father and mother."

How should we suppose that the only Man who is able to keep that commandment perfectly feels about His mother? Think about the way we poor, sinful humans respect our own dear mothers and defend their honor. What a glorious place must Mary have within her Son's perfectly loving, perfectly honoring heart!

So how disappointed must the Savior be when He hears someone who professes to love and follow Him demanding that His mother be treated as "nothing special"? How sorrowful is He over those who lovingly revere preachers, presidents, and football coaches, but deride those who honor His mother as He does? How pained is He for those who denigrate the precious woman who unselfishly opened her arms to Him, that He might pour forth His grace upon all mankind?

In the Orthodox Faith, we give Mary her just due when we venerate her with love and gratitude. She is not God. She is not our Savior. But she is that righteous, blessed woman through whom the Son of God entered the world, becoming Man. She is the one who willingly said "Yes!" to God, so that the rejecting "No!" that had resounded within the human race since the Fall might be forever silenced. She is the Mother of God. He chose her to be the one who bore Him. In all the universe, in all of Heaven, there is none other like her.

Indeed, all generations shall call her Blessed!

⇥ 17 ⇤

The Saints

Not only is Mary unique in the sight of God, but so are the saints.

The Psalmist declares, "*Precious* in the sight of the LORD / Is the death of His saints" (Psalm 116:15, italics mine). If we claim to love Christ, and wish to join our hearts to His, should not those who are precious to Him be also precious to us? All those blessed laborers who have struggled valiantly to advance the Gospel against the forces of darkness, who have performed miracles and wonders in the power of the Spirit, who have poured out their life blood for the sake of their beloved Master—these holy ones God Himself honors.

If we are surrounded by such a great cloud of witnesses (Hebrews 12:1), how can we ignore them?

As a Protestant, however, I found it quite easy to ignore them. I didn't, after all, want to be like the Roman Catholics. But in my lack of honor for those who have fought the good fight and finished the course, I demonstrated that cold-hearted, self-centered individualism that strangled the true spirit of love in my life.

Recently, I saw my old attitude illustrated in a conversation I had with a Protestant friend. Somehow, the story of the Samaritan woman at Jacob's well came up (see John 4). I mentioned to my friend that Church tradition tells us the woman's baptismal name was Photini, the "light-bearer," and that she was martyred some years after her conversion. My friend just chuckled derisively and said, "How do you know that's true? And more importantly, what difference does it make?"

My friend's dismissal was easy to understand. Knowing her name doesn't make any difference, when faith is only about rational spiritual principles that I try to apply in my life. When my Christianity is just about "Jesus and me," there's no reason to think about any-one but Him and myself. When my salvation is merely contractual, the satisfying of an angry Judge, other people don't really mean much. When my faith is mostly in my head instead of in my heart, what difference does it make that the woman's name was Photini?

But when my faith is about living in love with Christ and His Church, loving everything He loves, things are different. Photini is the name of a New Testament saint of God, precious to His Son, for she lives in His Presence. Her story goes like this: When she left that well, she spent a lifetime spreading the Good News. On a day that Christ and His Church remember well, she and her family marched boldly before the throne of the tyrant Nero and declared the Gospel to him. They went to their deaths fearlessly (tradition says they drowned Photini upside-down in a well) but not before they had converted many members of Nero's court. True to His promise, Jesus Christ received them into His Presence with joy and honor.

As an Orthodox Christian, my faith in Christ includes a rela-tionship with others who call upon His name—here in the Church or in Paradise. It is, from beginning to end, about *love*. My faith includes the love and knowledge of other people, not just prin-ciples. Salvation is the fulfillment of Jesus' prayer (John 17) that we be one with Him, and one with all those whom He loves.

So when I hear the name Photini, my heart is warmed. And moved. Within my soul I say, *This is my beloved and glorious sister, and I am so very proud of her.* Thinking of her, I am inspired with a longing to love Christ our God in the same self-sacrificing way she loves Him.

In our veneration of the saints, we Orthodox Christians are only expressing an attitude that has been alive in the Church since its earliest days. For instance, when Polycarp, Bishop of Smyrna, was martyred for Christ (around the year 150), a letter was sent out to all the churches, describing the noble death of this beloved man. The letter contains these words:

It is neither possible for us ever to forsake Christ, who suf-fered for the salvation of such as shall be saved throughout the whole world (the blameless one for sinners), nor to worship any other. For Him, indeed, as being the Son of God, we adore; *but the martyrs, as disciples and followers of the Lord, we worthily love* on account of their extraordinary affection towards their own King and Master, of whom may we also be made companions and fellow-disciples! (italics mine)[1]

Obviously, I can't "worthily love" others by disdaining all mention of them, or by ignoring them. If I decide to "worthily love" someone, how do I typically show it? Just by holding an occasional good thought toward them? No, usually we do things like embrace them, or—in the case of our most beloved ones—give them a kiss. How do you kiss a martyr (or some other extraordinary saint) who should be worthily loved? One way the Church has done it over the centuries is by venerating the saint's icon. It is as simple as that.

The State of the Departed
Now at this point, some of my Protestant friends may say, "Okay, it's fine to honor saints. But the real problem is, you ask them to pray for you. And they're dead! The Scriptures say communicating with the dead is an abomination (Deuteronomy 18:10, 11). So how can you justify what you do?"

Since I've become Orthodox, I've had this discussion about the saints numerous times. I've discovered there's a lot more variety in Protestant beliefs regarding the state of the departed than I ever realized before. So before I can talk about the legitimacy of invoking the saints in intercession, let me first address the nature of death.

I grew up in a denomination that believes the Scriptures are quite clear on what happens when you're dead. Essentially, you go to sleep. You remain in an entirely unconscious state until the Second Coming of Christ. This belief is based on some very straightforward Scriptures:

For the living know that they will die;
But the dead know nothing . . .

Nevermore will they have a share
In anything done under the sun.
(Ecclesiastes 9:5, 6)

The dead do not praise the LORD,
Nor any who go down into silence.
(Psalm 115:17)

The meaning of texts like these seemed so obvious that I never
questioned my belief until I was in my twenties, and one day read a
text that I had not noticed before. It is part of the "Kingdom Song"
of Israel, which we read in Isaiah 26:

Your dead shall live;
Together with my dead body they shall arise.
Awake and sing, you who dwell in dust;
For your dew is like the dew of herbs,
And the earth shall cast out the dead.
(Isaiah 26:19, italics mine)

Initially, I saw this verse as consistent with my beliefs about the
state of the dead. I figured it referred to the final resurrection at the
Judgment. But then I took note of the words that I've italicized.
God is the One who speaks these words. When does He say that the
dead of Israel, those who "know nothing" and who "do not praise
the LORD," will live again? With the rising of "my dead body." Thus,
this cannot be a reference to a resurrection at the end of time. Since
the words come from God's mouth, it is a clear reference to Christ's
own Resurrection from the dead.

Then I recognized that this passage is a specific prophecy about
the event recounted in Matthew 27:52, 53: "And the graves were
opened; and many bodies of the saints who had fallen asleep were
raised; and coming out of the graves after His resurrection, they
went into the holy city and appeared to many."

But reading Isaiah 26, it is clear that the promises being made
are not just for a small group of individuals. This prophecy is

completely general; it is for the entirety of God's people. So I realized that in some sense, Christ's Resurrection brought life to all the dead—not at the final Judgment, but in the hour of His rising. For as the passage says, the dead rise together with His dead body.

Thus, I was forced to take a hard look at what had always been a pretty cut-and-dried subject for me. All the texts that supported my view of the state of the dead were from the Old Testament. From what I was reading in Isaiah 26, it became obvious to me that with Christ's conquering of death, the state of the dead changes! For the first time, I realized this was a perfectly reasonable assumption. For when something is vanquished, isn't it typically the case that its power is dissolved? The oddest outcome imaginable would be for Jesus to conquer death, only to have everything about death stay exactly as it was before He overcame it!

Once I began to entertain the thought that the state of the dead might be different since the Resurrection of Christ, many texts in the New Testament started to make more sense to me. Read through St. Paul's words to the Corinthians and to the Philippians on the matter:

> For we who are in this tent groan, being burdened, not because we want to be unclothed, but further clothed, that mortality may be swallowed up by life. Now He who has prepared us for this very thing is God, who has also given us the Spirit as a guarantee. So we are always confident, knowing that *while we are at home in the body we are absent from the Lord.* For we walk by faith, not by sight. We are confident, yes, well pleased rather *to be absent from the body and to be present with the Lord.* Therefore we make it our aim, whether present or absent, to be well pleasing to Him (2 Corinthians 5:4–9, italics mine).

> For to me, to live is Christ, and to die is gain. But if I live on in the flesh, this will mean fruit from my labor; yet what I shall choose I cannot tell. For I am hard pressed between the two, *having a desire to depart and be with Christ, which is*

far better. Nevertheless to remain in the flesh is more needful for you (Philippians 1:21–24, italics mine).

When I believed the dead to be in a thoroughly unconscious state, these verses were troubling for me. First of all, if one is not here in the body, Paul says, then one is "present with the Lord." It makes no sense whatsoever that Paul would use the term "present with the Lord" to describe a situation in which he actually would be totally oblivious to whether or not he were "present" or "with the Lord."

Also, Paul says that in that state of "being present" with the Lord, he would desire to be well pleasing to Him. How could Paul possibly "aim" to be "well pleasing" to Christ in a state of unconsciousness? Aiming at something and doing it are without question conscious activities.

The Philippians text was even more troubling. Paul is having a crisis born of love. He is struggling between his longing to be with Christ, and his concern for Christ's Church. But when I rephrase this text in a way consistent with a belief that the dead exist in an unconscious state, Paul's dilemma no longer seems like one of love: "For I am hard pressed to choose between staying alive a while longer in order to love and care for you, my dear ones, and what I really want: to die and spend perhaps ages in a state of sleep, waiting to be in the presence of Christ (although to me, the passage of that time will seem like only a moment)."

If St. Paul and the early Church viewed death this way, then as a member of the Philippian church, I'd be offended at the Apostle's sarcasm. His plain message would be that he had pretty much had it with his ministry. He'd rather pass his time in a state of unconsciousness than stay here and continue to deal with folks like me. I mean, why else would he choose "going to sleep" over remaining with his people?

According to this view, the time between death and becoming conscious of Christ seems like a moment, no matter how long it actually is. So why is St. Paul so reluctant to stay a few more years, unless he's tired, or just doesn't care anymore? Was he such a purely selfish existentialist? No, because the truth is, the Apostle Paul expected to be with the Christ he loved as soon as he passed beyond this mortal life.

However, the text that really came alive, once I began to see that death was no longer a state of unconsciousness, was Hebrews 12:22–24. In this passage, as members of Christ's Body here on earth, we

> *have come* to Mount Zion and to the city of the living God, the heavenly Jerusalem, to an innumerable company of angels, to *the general assembly* and *church of the firstborn* who are registered in heaven, to God the Judge of all, *to the spirits of just men made perfect*, to Jesus the Mediator of the new covenant, and to the blood of sprinkling that speaks better things than that of Abel (italics mine).

Note the past tense here. We "have come" to Mount Zion. So *right now*, not in some future age, the Church on earth is joined with the Church in heaven. These heavenly and earthly contingents form one unified Body of Christ. The Church is not composed of angels—though they are present, too. No, it is made up of human beings who have been purchased by the blood of Jesus Christ. The "firstborn" of these believers, now living in heaven, are described as "the spirits of just men made perfect." Is unconsciousness a trait of a "perfect" man? Clearly not. These just men are "assembled," along with us.

For what one purpose does the Church come together? To worship Jesus—something that those perfect men could not do as mindless souls passing their time in oblivion.

The Verdict Is In

But the final mind-changing clincher came when I began to read early Church writings for myself. There, I discovered perfectly plain teachings as to what the Apostolic Church believed about the state of the dead. I've already mentioned the letter (circa 150) that described the martyrdom of Polycarp, Bishop of Smyrna.

The entire Church loved Polycarp. He had come to Christ

through the preaching of the Apostle John and was a devoted spiritual child of that Beloved Disciple. The Church of Polycarp's day held in highest esteem those few, precious surviving links to the Apostles. Thus, all were interested in hearing the details of his martyrdom. Toward the end of this letter, one reads:

> This, then, is the account of the blessed Polycarp, who, being the twelfth that was martyred at Smyrna . . . yet occupies a place of his own in the memory of all men. . . . For, having through patience overcome the unjust governor, and thus acquired the crown of immortality, *he now with the apostles and all the righteous (in heaven), rejoicingly glorifies God,* even the Father, and blesses the Lord Jesus Christ, the Saviour of our souls, the Governor of our bodies, and the Shepherd of the Catholic Church throughout the world (italics mine).[2]

It was impossible for me to believe that those who had been taught by St. Polycarp, who had himself been taught the Faith by the Beloved John, would not have it straight regarding apostolic teaching as to what happens to us after death. Nor could I believe that the rest of the churches would not have raised a fuss when they got this letter, if the Smyrnaeans had been proclaiming heretical doctrine regarding the state of the dead.

Thus, I began to uncover the ancient, Apostolic Church's understanding of death. I learned that prior to the Resurrection, the souls of the dead had waited silently in the grave. Because Jesus had not yet opened the way to heaven, men could not be rewarded—either for their godliness or for their wickedness. They remained firmly in the silent clutches of God's great enemy, death. This is the state of the world that the Old Testament texts on death describe.

But at the Resurrection, death was entirely defeated. Oh, it still exists, awaiting its destruction at the Judgment (1 Corinthians 15:24–26). But no longer does it have any dominion over us (Romans 6:8, 9). Death no longer has the power to end our lives, or to steal our consciousness. Thus St. Paul could warmly anticipate a real and intimate encounter with his precious Lord when the chapter of his earthly sojourn was closed. He, like the thief on the cross and all those who have departed trusting in Christ, awaits the Judgment in the Paradise of His Presence. Those who have hated Him await that Judgment in the darkness of His absence.

When we have grasped the truth about death, calling on the intercessions of Mary and the saints is an absolutely natural thing to do. Clearly, since the Resurrection, the Old Testament's blanket prohibitions on communing with the dead are not applicable. In Old Testament times, those who would talk to the dead were trying to contact spirits whom God had given over to the silent, unconscious bondage of death. Any attempt to reach them represented disobedience and defiance toward God and a submission to the powers of darkness.

But in His rising, Jesus Himself set mankind free from that dark, still prison of Hades. Thus, the only meaning that the word "dead" can have when applied to Mary and the departed saints is simply, "They do not live *here* anymore." For having taken up their abode with Christ in eternity, they are more alive than they have ever been. According to Hebrews 12, they are "perfect"! As one Body, we worship Christ together with them. Together we glory in His total victory over the devil and his ultimate weapon, death. Jesus has vanquished death by destroying the barrier between this earthly realm and the spiritual Kingdom—between this world of struggle and our eternal home.

Living in the Spiritual Realm

Thus, no separation or isolation may be drawn between the Church *visible* upon earth and the Church *invisible* in Heaven. With death's power gone, there is no wall between them. When Christ looks upon his worshiping Church, He sees one Body. His earthly servants stand shoulder-to-shoulder with those who have gone on before us to their rest.

St. Paul certainly sees things that way. In 2 Timothy 1:16–18, he intercedes for a departed saint. Onesiphorus, a good Christian friend who met the Apostle in Rome, has passed away. St. Paul prays that the Lord will "grant to him that he may find mercy from the Lord in that Day [the Day of Judgment]" (v. 18).

So ultimately, the difference between an Orthodox Christian and a Protestant, with regard to the saints or in any other matter, is essentially this: In all things, we Orthodox Christians see the world through Jesus' eyes, and not our own. He sees our departed brethren as alive and joined with us in worship of Him. Thus, we must see them that way, and act toward them accordingly.

The spiritual world is the real world. This temporal world in which we live is fading fast, and one day will be no more. True reality, and true life, can be found only where Jesus abides. Hebrews 12 makes it clear that He dwells in "Mount Zion," the "heavenly Jerusalem." Not only is this where we believers shall spend eternity; as St. Paul states clearly, that is where we are now—in the most real way imaginable.

If one is to be a spiritual person, and know Christ as Christ would be known, he must open his heart to these powerful realities. He must live in them. This is why we Orthodox commune with the saints. To be sure, we do not conduct séances, or invoke the intercessions of every departed aunt, uncle, and cousin we can think of. We clearly recognize there is such a thing as evil spiritism.

That's why, as in all other things Orthodox, it is the consensus of the Church, not just your opinion or mine, that determines who is worthy of sainthood and veneration. The clear witness of the Holy Spirit among the clergy and laity alike is the key factor here.

Not of This World
But what do you say to those who warn us of the "spiritual danger" of honoring and calling upon the saints of the Church for intercession? To ignore and forget them would be playing right into the hands of the devil. For what has always been his hold over us? Our fear of death! The Scriptures teach us that the "fear of death" has kept us in bondage to Satan our entire lives (Hebrews 2:15). What happens to us, then, if we shy away in fear from that world beyond the grave, from that realm where Christ and His true Church live?

When the devil can get us to ignore *that* world, either from fear or lack of interest, our only alternative is to devote our attention fully to the *here* of our present earthly existence. Rooting ourselves firmly in this world leads to loving this world and doing the sinful things that cause life in this world to thrive. At this, Satan and the demons rejoice.

Further, the Church Fathers encourage us to contemplate our own death, to prayerfully embrace its reality. As we do that, the heavenly Kingdom becomes more than a concept, more than a hope. We are seated with Christ in heavenly places. Living in the actuality of that realm beyond our sight, which includes the spiritual fellowship of the saints who dwell there, we establish ourselves with our true family and homeland.

By contrast, in disregarding the saints, we ignore those who have attained the prize. We thereby shut ourselves off from any insight regarding the manner of life we must follow in order to live where they live. We cannot avail ourselves of the great assistance that those gone before us can provide.

Sadly, the disease of individualism drives us modern Christians to try to make it all on our own. When we do not allow ourselves to touch that spiritual Kingdom where Christ and His saints dwell, Christianity becomes a spiritually sanitized rendition of secular, temporal existence. If we shut our eyes to the realm where the saints dwell, even the most sincere believers will have no comprehension of what it means to be in the world, but not of it.

Let us as Orthodox believers not let the devil have his way. May we choose to recognize our holy brethren of the Church triumphant, and live with them in that victory of love, the Resurrection of Christ, which transcends the world. Our departed and victorious brethren lead us to the Master's outstretched arms. They encourage us as we walk with Him. They train us to run the race set before us. They show us how to bow in submission to Christ our God.

So let us rejoice and together glorify Christ, whose power has destroyed the veil between the worlds. And let us live in love with Him, and all the brethren, now and ever, and unto the ages of ages. Amen.

→ 18 ←

To Be Orthodox

As I bring this book to a close, I am prayerfully hopeful for many things. I pray that Protestant readers have been challenged to come to grips with the inescapable inconsistencies of their theological heritage. I hope that many of their misconceptions regarding the ancient Orthodox Faith have been dispelled. Most of all, I hope I have helped them to see Christianity in the light of its historical truth and its sacramental spirit.

When it comes to Orthodox readers, my prayer is that this book has nurtured within them a deeper appreciation of their faith. Perhaps they have come to understand it better. Most of all, I hope that they will be able to use the perspectives presented here to help them as they share the truth of their faith in a predominantly Protestant society.

So what remains to be said? Only this: It is not enough that this book may have persuaded a Protestant reader to admit, "The teachings of the Orthodox Church are true." It is not enough that the words on these pages have filled an Orthodox reader with a deeper conviction that his or her beliefs are right.

No, this book will not have accomplished its work unless it has encouraged its readers—both Protestant and Orthodox—to really *be* Orthodox. For the Orthodox Faith is not a philosophy to which one gives mental assent. It is not merely a set of doctrines that one chooses to believe. No, Orthodoxy is a sacramental life that must be lived out within the communal bonds of the true Body of Christ. It is a life totally devoted to the self-sacrificing, obedient service of Christ. Through that wholehearted and complete obedience, one participates in the breath, heartbeat, movement, desire, and Spirit of the living Christ.

The Challenge
Again, let me be clear that the challenge to be Orthodox is a gauntlet thrown down to all of us—to honest-hearted Protestants who are for the first time confronting the truths of the ancient Faith, and to those of us who already bear the name "Orthodox."

You see, as sad as it is to admit, many of us Orthodox fail miserably when it comes to living the Faith. Although we hold the truth of the ages in our hands, we all too easily ignore it. Too often we just go through the motions of the sacramental life, and pay lip service to the truths of the Faith. We don't really let it change us and free us. We don't let it work in us the "mystery of godliness" (1 Timothy 3:16).

This lamentable fact is revealed in the coldness and apathy that one feels in some Orthodox churches. Even more tragically, it displays itself in bitter contentions and rivalries, in the deep and ugly wounds that we Orthodox sometimes mercilessly and self-righteously inflict on the hearts and souls of our brothers and sisters. It manifests itself in those internal schisms that debilitate churches and shipwreck the spiritual lives of those caught up in the waves of divisiveness.

These are not new evils in the Church, obviously. The New Testament shows us that the Body of Christ has faced such struggles from its beginning. But these problems become extremely poignant in a time when so many hearts are thirsting for the healing waters of original Christianity. When we Orthodox exhibit such un-Orthodox behavior, all the while claiming to be heirs of the Apostolic Faith, we do nothing to help seekers find their way to the truth. In fact, we may very well turn them away from it. What a terrible responsibility to bear.

As Orthodox Christians, we know the truth. And we *know* that we know it. What, then, can be done for us when we place that truth on a shelf and live according to our own self-centered agendas? Contemplating this, I am soberly reminded of the words of Jesus: "To whom much is given, from him much will be required" (Luke 12:48). All I can say is, Lord Jesus Christ, have mercy on us all.

The Obstacle and the Remedy

And, praise to His Name, He does. The Lord provides a remedy for the apathetic Orthodox whose life denies the Faith. It is the same remedy that is held forth to the Protestant who longs to know God, but who also knows that he hasn't really found the way to do that. Healing and transformation will come for both, as each responds to the call to *be* Orthodox. The grace of God resides in that call, empowering those who take it to heart. The one who heeds it will experience the true love of Christ. But he must embrace the *whole* of the ancient Faith, and *practice* its truths diligently.

In our attempts to do this, Protestant seekers and Orthodox strugglers face a common obstacle. The impediment is a powerful misconception regarding the nature of Christianity. It was given birth in the Great Schism, nursed by the Reformation, nurtured by the Enlightenment, and brought to full maturity in the atmosphere of liberalism and self-centered individuality that defines our modern culture.

The misconception is this: Christianity is essentially a faith that one can individually interpret and apply as one pleases. To many, the myriads of Christian denominations, rather than being a sign that something is dreadfully wrong in Christendom, instead testify to the fact that there are many paths to Christ. In their minds, it's perfectly obvious that a person is free to choose whatever path suits his personal needs, desires, and tastes. If one doesn't like any of the existing paths, he can legitimately create his own.

Again, many of us Orthodox, as well as Protestants, buy that line to one degree or another. But I can tell you this: If I proposed that definition of the Christian life to Christians of the apostolic age, or to Christians of subsequent ages who remained true to the apostolic faith, they would call me nonsensical—maybe even brand me a heretic. To them, the words of the Apostle would be eminently clear: To be called a Christian, one must "stand fast and hold the traditions" of the Faith, as they have been taught from the beginning (2 Thessalonians 2:15). Only those who embrace "that faith which has been believed everywhere, always, by all"[1] can genuinely bear the name of Christ.

Thus, true Christianity has no room for personal interpretations, preferences, qualifications, exemptions, or adjustments. Anyone, Protestant or Orthodox, who wants to enter into a real relationship with Jesus Christ must accept the fact that the Faith of the Apostles preserved in Holy Orthodoxy is an historical reality, not just a theological school of thought. We must not forget that until the eleventh century, "to be a Christian" meant "to be Orthodox." Of course, that's the point I've been arguing in this book. But I'll reiterate here that once a person accepts the fact that it is history, and not our personal interpretation of the Scriptures, that tells us what the Christian Faith is, the fact that Orthodoxy is the one true expression of that Faith is fairly easy to discover.

We must also understand that the Faith has not been bequeathed to us in order that it may serve us. Rather, we are all called to serve it. We are all priests of the New Covenant in Christ Jesus, required to offer up "spiritual sacrifices acceptable to God" (1 Peter 2:9). As priests, we are not called to create the Faith. Instead, we are enjoined to keep *all* its tenets, and observe *all* its sacraments. These we must observe faithfully—not as empty rituals and mindless doctrines, but as the essential steps in the mysterious and miraculous dance of love that Jesus Himself has choreographed for us.

Still, the attitude of the age is mesmerizing; and so both Protestant seekers and Orthodox stumblers may succumb to the self-seeking spirit that sweet-talks us into believing that we ourselves are the determiners of truth. Rather than presenting himself to the demands of the Ancient Faith unreservedly, as "a living sacrifice" (Romans 12:1), one seduced by the modern spirit may instead feel perfectly justified in modifying the Faith, or even wholly rejecting it.

That's why we find Protestant seekers who stop at the doorway of the Church because they don't want to go to confession, or they find venerating icons distasteful, or the idea of living in obedience to a spiritual father or bishop just rubs their independent souls the wrong way. It could be any one of a host of issues. These folks may be convinced of the historical truth of Orthodoxy. They may even agree with much of what the Faith teaches. But sadly, they will feel absolutely justified in rejecting it if it doesn't perfectly match their personal views of what Christianity ought to be.

Regrettably, this is not a problem only for Protestant seekers. Many of us Orthodox Christians do the same kind of thing. We decide we just don't want to fast or go to confession. We ignore—maybe even resent—those in spiritual authority over us. We willingly let football games and weekends at the lake take priority over worship of the Holy Trinity. Why? Because personally, we just don't feel those things are all that necessary.

Now, the spirit of the age would have us all believe that it's actually God's will that we exercise our "spiritual freedom" in this way. Its deceptive voice would convince us that the way we practice our Christian faith should be—no, *must* be—conformed to our own will, and to our own tastes. God's primary concern, the *zeitgeist* assures us, is that we be individually comfortable in our faith. If we don't find a practice or belief personally meaningful, then we should not feel obligated to it.

Who Is the Judge?

In stark contrast to this self-centered spirit stands the ancient Orthodox Faith. If there is one thing that must be learned by the Protestant seeking truth, and the Orthodox desiring to live the fullness of the Faith, it is this: *We have no right to judge the Faith. Rather, it is the Faith that must judge us.* If it tells us we are wrong, we must admit it. What it calls us to do and believe, we must do and believe with all our hearts. This is what it means to be Orthodox.

Of course, another reason Protestant seekers sometimes balk at coming into the Faith, and the reason that many of us Orthodox find it too easy to ignore important aspects of our Faith, is that the true Faith is so incredibly demanding. It asks of us very difficult things.

In this, the Ancient Faith runs hard against the grain of the spirit of this age. It doesn't ask us to come under its authority so that we can find a warm, comfortable, meaningful faith that fits our lifestyle. Instead, it calls us to fast, to weep bitterly for our sins, to deny our personal pleasures and comforts, to yield to spiritual authority, to mistrust our own judgments, to genuinely forgive the unforgivable, and to honestly love the unlovable. In short, it calls us to live a life that is entirely "not of this world" (John 18:36).

God does not encumber us with these hard tasks in order to somehow make our lives miserable. No, they are necessary in order for us to experience our metamorphosis from sin-sick creatures into the beautiful Christlike beings He intends us to be. What's more, every person who finally decides to walk this Orthodox path discovers that until he embraced this way of tears and self-denial, he had never really tasted the true joy and peace of God's love. It's simple, really. Only in the depths of repentance and brokenness does one encounter the true magnitude of God's mercy and compassion. And the more ways one can find to deny his earthly self, the more room he makes in his heart for the divine Christ.

But this understanding of things has dramatically faded in the world. Our vision has become clouded, blurred by rationalism and errant doctrines like *sola scriptura*. Under the influence of these, the admonition of the Apostle Paul that we "not be conformed to this world" (Romans 12:1) has been reinterpreted. Tragically, we have come to believe that "good" doctrine and "good" worship are measured by how well they fit with "where we are personally"—or in other words, by how closely they conform to our own opinions, tastes, and desires.

St. Paul says that Jesus has "raised us up together, and made us sit together in the heavenly places" with Himself (Ephesians 2:6). If there is one obvious fact in the universe, it's that heaven is not like *here*. So if we are living the heavenly lives to which Christ has called us, it stands to reason they should stand out in vivid contrast to the world around us. The way we think, eat, sleep, love, worship, work, play—absolutely every aspect of our lives should be markedly different from the practices of those in the world. A life that is just Christian words set to the same old worldly tune cannot pass as the "transformed" life to which we are called (Romans 12:2).

Will He Find Faith?
When I was an evangelical Protestant, I used to puzzle over Jesus'

question, "When the Son of Man comes, will He really find faith on the earth?" (Luke 18:8). I mean, I'd look around at all the active churches, listen to the ever-expanding number of Christian radio shows, hear all the Christian bands (even on secular stations!), and tune in to the various Christian television networks. With all that activity exploding on the landscape of these last days, how could Jesus ever have posed such a question?

Perhaps He was looking on this broken and misguided age, where the true Faith has been almost entirely obscured by a thousand years of erroneous teachings. Maybe He was envisioning this world in which people have grown unable to trust anything but their own personal opinions. Perhaps He was peering into this time when men would confidently make themselves the judges of truth, and somehow manage to convince themselves that God wants it that way.

I see the stain of this corruption on the Protestant world. I see it on the Orthodox world. I see it on the Roman Catholic world. I see it on my own soul.

Yes, these are spiritually perilous times, but I am not anxious. For I have tasted the transforming power of Christ. Through the power of the Ancient Faith, I have encountered Him in ways that I never dreamed possible as a Protestant. All around me, I see large numbers of honest souls coming to the fountain of Orthodoxy and finding there the end to thirsty years of searching. In my heart, I know there are even greater days coming. I believe that Jesus will soon mightily challenge the darkness and raise the standard of Orthodoxy high and brightly over this spiritually confused world.

Sometimes I dare to envision a Sunday morning when every church in the land is filled with the sounds of the Divine Liturgy; when every bell tower rings out the song of unity—the hymn of the One True Faith; when the millions of worshiping hearts are joined in one Body—one with Christ, and one with each other; when the earth shakes and the demons tremble before the majestic glory of Christ's Holy, Undivided Church.

It has been a thousand years since Jesus has seen such a day. I know He longs to see it come again. My dear reader, let us *all* be Orthodox.

→ Notes ←

Introduction

1. In a report on growth during the 1990s, the *1995 Britannica Book of the Year* (Chicago: Encyclopaedia Britannica, Inc., 1995, p. 275) identified the average yearly growth rates for major Christian groups as follows: Roman Catholics, 0.65%; Protestants (all denominations overall), 0.49%; evangelical Protestants, 1.33%; Orthodox, 2.41%.

Chapter 5

1. Acts 13 relates the story of the sending forth of Saul (Paul) and Barnabas as missionaries from Antioch. In verse 2, we are told that the brethren "ministered to the Lord and fasted." The word "ministered" is the Greek *leitourgeo*, which means "to perform ritual acts" and is the root of the word "liturgy."

In this liturgical worship, the believers at Antioch were only following the precedent set by the Apostles and the first believers in Jerusalem. Acts 2:42 says that those first Christians participated together in the "breaking of bread" and "in prayers." Any Protestant who remembers the popular Communion song "Let Us Break Bread Together" knows that "breaking bread" is a reference to the Eucharist. The Greek phrase that is translated "in prayers" is actually more correctly rendered "in *the* prayers." This is a reference to the Jewish practice of formal, liturgical prayer services, in which those in the newly formed Church continued to participate. In fact, a few verses later, in Acts 3:1, we find Peter and John going up to the temple for the prayers of "the ninth hour." This was a well-defined liturgical service that was performed at 3:00 P.M. There were also services at the first hour (6:00 A.M.), third hour (9:00 A.M.), and sixth hour (12:00 P.M.). The early Church adopted this practice of liturgical prayer services; the "Hours" are still prayed in Orthodox monasteries, and in parishes where logistics permit. To these services, the early Church also added Vespers (6:00 P.M.), Compline (9:00 P.M.), Nocturnes (12:00 A.M.), and Matins (3:00 A.M.). To say that the Orthodox life is one of prayer is certainly an understatement.

See also St. Justin Martyr, *First Apology*, Chapter LXVII, in *Ante-Nicene Fathers*, Volume 1 (Christian Classics Ethereal Library: http://www. ccel. org/fathers2/).

2. Ignatius, *Epistle to the Smyrnaeans*, in *Ante-Nicene Fathers*, edited by Alexander Roberts and James Donaldson (Peabody, Massachusetts: Hendrickson Publishers, 1995), Vol. 1, p. 89.

Subsequent citations of this multi-volume work will be listed as *Ante-Nicene Fathers*.

3. *The Martyrdom of Polycarp*, chs. XVII and IX, in *Ante-Nicene Fathers*, Vol. 1, p. 43.

4. Origen, *Commentary on the Letter to the Romans* (5:19), quoted in "Infant Baptism," by John W. Hardenbrook, Conciliar Press, 1994, pp. 10, 11. See also Migne, J. P., ed., *Patrologiae Graeca*, Vol. 14, 1047B.

Chapter 6

1. St. Ignatius was ordained as the second bishop of Antioch in the year 69. Around the turn of the first century, he was taken to Rome and martyred for his beloved Christ. Ignatius was converted under the preaching of the Apostles, and served faithfully as one of their first successors. He was renowned and loved throughout the entire Church. In a letter written on his way to Rome to die, he says this regarding the Sabbath:

If, then, those who were conversant with the ancient Scriptures came to newness of hope, expecting the coming of Christ . . . how shall we be able to live without Him? The prophets were His servants, and foresaw Him by the Spirit, and waited for Him as . . . their Lord and Saviour, saying, "He will come and save us." Let us therefore no longer keep the Sabbath after the Jewish manner, and rejoice in days of idleness; for "he that does not work, let him not eat." . . . But let every one of you keep the Sabbath after a spiritual manner, rejoicing in meditation on the law, not in relaxation of the body, admiring the workmanship of God, and not eating things prepared the day before, nor using lukewarm drinks, and walking within a prescribed space, nor finding delight in dancing and plaudits which have no sense in them. And after observance of the Sabbath, let every friend of Christ keep the Lord's Day, as a festival, the resurrection-day, the queen and chief of all the [days of the week]. Looking forward to this, the prophet declared, "To the end, for the eighth day," on which our life both sprang up again, and the victory over death was obtained in Christ, whom the children of perdition, the enemies of the Saviour, deny. (See *Ante-Nicene Fathers*, Vol. 1, pp. 62, 63.)

2. St. Vincent of Lerins, *A Commonitory,* Chapter II.6, in *A Select Library of Nicene and Post-Nicene Fathers of the Christian Church,* P. Schaff and H. Wace, editors (New York: The Christian Literature Company, 1894), volume XI, p. 132.

3. See Mastrantonis, George, *Augsburg and Constantinople* (Brookline, Massachusetts: Holy Cross Orthodox Press, 1982).

Chapter 7

1. Some Protestant confessions are sacramental in nature. For the problems inherent in Protestant sacramentalism, see p. 92.

2. Lewis, C. S., *The Screwtape Letters* (New York: Simon & Schuster, First Touchstone Edition, 1996), p. 29.

3. Early in the second century, St. Sophia was martyred with her three young daughters. As they faced unspeakable tortures, she encouraged them with these words:

Your heavenly Lover, Jesus Christ, is eternal health, inexpressible beauty and life eternal. When your bodies are slain by torture, He will clothe you in incorruption and the wounds on your bodies will shine in heaven like the stars.

See Velimirovic, Bishop Nikolai, *The Prologue from Ochrid,* translated by Mother Maria (Birmingham, England: Lazarica Press, 1985), Volume 3, p. 340.

Chapter 9

1. See above, Chapter 5, note 1.

2. St. Justin Martyr, *First Apology,* Chapter LXVII, in *Ante-Nicene Fathers,* Volume 1. (Christian Classics Ethereal Library, http: //www. ccel. org/fathers2/.)

Chapter 11

1. Irenaeus, *Against Heresies*, Book II, 22:4, in *Ante-Nicene Fathers,* Vol. 1, p. 391.

2. Origen, *Commentary on the Letter to the Romans* (5:19), quoted in "Infant Baptism," by John W. Hardenbrook, Conciliar Press, 1994, pp. 10, 11. See also Migne, J. P., ed., *Patrologiae Graeca*, Vol. 14, 1047B.

3. Cyprian, *Epistle LVIII*, in *Ante-Nicene Fathers*, Vol. V, p. 354.

Chapter 13

1. Ignatius, *Epistle to the Smyrnaeans*, in *Ante-Nicene Fathers*, Vol. 1, p. 89. (For full bibliographic reference, see Chapter 5, note 2.)

Chapter 15

1. Lewis, C. S., *The Screwtape Letters* (New York: Simon & Schuster, First Touchstone Edition, 1996), pp. 28, 29.

2. Sakharov, Archimandrite Sophrony, *St. Silouan the Athonite* (Crestwood, NY: St. Vladimir's Seminary Press, 1999), p. 292.

3. *Op. cit.,* p. 69.

Chapter 17

1. *The Martyrdom of Polycarp*, Ch. XVII, in *Ante-Nicene Fathers*, Vol. 1, p. 43.

2. *Op. cit.,* Ch. XIX.

Chapter 18

1. St. Vincent of Lerins, *A Commonitory,* in *A Select Library of Nicene and Post-Nicene Fathers of the Christian Church,* volume XI, p. 132. (For full bibliographic reference, see Chapter 6, note 2.)

Other stories of people who have embraced the Orthodox Faith:

NEARLY ORTHODOX
by Angela Doll Carlson
From Catholic schoolgirl to punk rocker to emergent church planter, Angela Doll Carlson traveled a spiritual path that in many ways mirrors that of a whole generation. She takes us with her on a deep and revealing exploration of the forces that drove her toward Orthodoxy and the challenges that long kept her from fully entering in.
ISBN: 978-1-936270-96-5

BECOMING ORTHODOX
by Fr. Peter E. Gillquist
The inspiring story of over two thousand evangelical Christians and their search for historic Christianity. This book is for evangelical Christians on their own search for the Church. It is also for Orthodox Christians looking for renewal.
ISBN: 978-1-936270-00-2

SURPRISED BY CHRIST
by V. Rev. A. James Bernstein
Raised in Queens, New York, by formerly Orthodox Jewish parents whose faith had been undermined by the Holocaust, Arnold Bernstein went on his own personal quest for spiritual meaning. He was ready to accept God in whatever form He chose to reveal Himself—and that turned out to be Christ. But Bernstein soon perceived discrepancies in the various forms of Protestant belief that surrounded him, and so his quest continued—this time for the true Church.
ISBN: 978-1-888212-95-2

AT THE CORNER OF EAST AND NOW
by Frederica Mathewes-Green
Acclaimed author Frederica Mathewes-Green takes us through a typical Divine Liturgy in her little parish of Holy Cross in Baltimore, setting of her well-loved book *Facing East*. Interspersed with reflections on the liturgy and the Orthodox faith are accounts of adventures around the country. In all the places she visits and all the people she meets, Frederica finds insights about faith, American life, and what it means to be human, and she shares these insights with wit, pathos, and folksy friendliness.
ISBN: 978-1-888212-34-1

TOUCHING HEAVEN
by John Oliver
"Deep in a northern Russian forest of jade and brown, far from any hint of civilization, Valaam Monastery sinks into the seasons of the year as it has for a thousand years

before. . . ." So begins the story of John Oliver, a young evangelical American on a journey of discovery—a journey that leads him to an ancient Russian monastery, a place of peace and a place of struggle. For on Valaam, he encounters Orthodox Christianity and is reminded that the Christian life is not for the faint of heart. And on Valaam, the treasure of stillness requires a fierce guarding.
ISBN: 978-1-888212-65-5

COMING HOME
Edited by Fr. Peter E. Gillquist
Eighteen testimonies from former Protestant clergy of diverse backgrounds—Presbyterian, Baptist, United Methodist, charismatic, Anglican, and more—who are uniting under the banner of the One Holy and Apostolic Church.
ISBN: 978-0-9622713-8

OUR HEARTS' TRUE HOME
Edited by Virginia Nieuwsma
Presents fourteen warm, inspiring stories of women coming into the Orthodox Faith. These women come from a wide variety of backgrounds, yet there's a common thread: no matter how they struggled, their journeys are infused with the love and mercy of God.
ISBN: 978-1-888212-02-0

To request a catalog, to obtain complete ordering information, or to place a credit card order, please call us at (800) 967-7377 or (219) 728-2216 or log onto our website: store.ancientfaith.com.

Ancient Faith Publishing hopes you have enjoyed and benefited from this book. The proceeds from the sales of our books only partially cover the costs of operating our nonprofit ministry—which includes both the work of **Ancient Faith Publishing** (formerly known as Conciliar Press) and the work of **Ancient Faith Radio**. Your financial support makes it possible to continue this ministry both in print and online. Donations are tax-deductible and can be made at www.ancientfaith.com.

Bringing you Orthodox Christian music, readings, prayers, teaching and podcasts 24 hours a day since 2004 at
www.ancientfaith.com

CPSIA information can be obtained at www.ICGtesting.com
Printed in the USA
LVOW08s1041280416

485738LV00004B/115/P